The Shift

Step into the *POWER* of your *POTENTIAL*

The
Spirit Spa
Press™

The Shift Café

Step into the *POWER* of your *POTENTIAL*

CINDY ALLEN-STUCKEY
With **Karen Packwood**

The Spirit Spa

London

The Spirit Spa Press Ltd

3rd Floor
86-90 Paul Street,
London
EC2A 4NE

First Paperback Edition Published 2022

A catalogue record for this book is available from the British Library.

ISBN: 978-1-7396207-0-7

Illustrations copyright © Emily Woodthorpe 2022
Front cover illustration : © Cindy Allen-Stuckey 2022
Typesetting and book cover design by Tara-Lee York Designs™

The
Spirit Spa
Press™

thespiritspapress.com

For my mother and great-aunt Florence

Praise for *The Shift Cafe*

'*The Shift Café was truly one of my blessings.*' **Christy, Indiana, USA**

'*Each exercise is simple yet powerful – easy to fit into my week yet adding instant value to my happiness. Thank you!*' **Claire, Lincoln, UK**

'*The content of the book is perfect for professional women's groups or women's book clubs*'. **Colette, Indiana, USA**

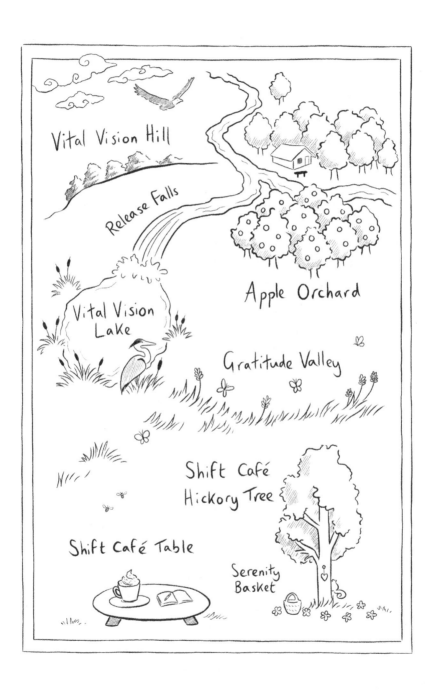

A Reminder of Who I Am.

(A Note to Myself)

by *Karen Packwood*

 I forgot

who I once was, who I am

what I want, what I need.

I was knocked from my perch

by nerves and self-doubt.

As I saw others securing their dreams, insecurity swept through me.

Where's mine? I wondered.

I became tired of jumping from the cliffs of my life, falling to my destiny not

knowing if, how or when my own pathway would catch me. Tired of landing

on the runway of my life crumpled by negativity and fear.

Exhausted   Angry   Jealous

… a withering mess of despondency …

I forgot

who I once was, who I am,

what I want, what I need.

I took my eyes from the ball of my life and became …distracted.

Forgot to breathe into the beauty of my power.

And discovered that it was hell. To forget.

To lose myself in the despair of seeing others achieve while I was still

scrambling up the scree, with blooded knees,

to the summit of my own mountain

Yet when the exhaustion and despair finally tired itself (and it truly did), I remembered
who I once was, who I now am,
what I want, what I need.

I am ...

Mother, Lover
Wild Woman
Storyteller
Fire Walker
Mountain Climber
Adventurer
Risk Taker

For one long moment I forgot and in the forgetting I fell.
Yet today, as the wind blows through the trees and rivers babble, I remember. I am ...

... a gentle and peaceful woman with great strength and deep wisdom who is about to get up from her knees, haul her backpack on her shoulders, take a deep breath and remember.
In this remembering, I will reach the summit of my life's mountain where I will, finally, step into the success of my own achievements ...

Who are you?
Have you forgotten who you once were, what you now need?
Or ...
Do you remember?

The Shift Café Menu

Contemplation Nook

Sip 1

Nurturing Quality Time

It's not that we have little time, but more that we waste a good deal of it.

Seneca

The Shift Café Definition of Nurturing

~⚬~❦~⚬~❦~⚬~❦~⚬~

To mindfully attain your life's dreams by nourishing them,
and yourself, with loving kindness, and compassion.

The Thaw

Imagine a mid-winter morning. Your gait is slow with the effort of trudging through fresh layers of thick snow that fell through the night. Despite your fleece coat, woolen gloves and fur-lined boots, the cold bites into your bones. Walking through a dense forest of snow laden trees you pause by the shore of a small lake. Peering onto the surface you notice how ice and the dark night make it impossible to see your reflection. You sigh. Even here you are unseen. You've been searching for a long time feeling lost and invisible, hopeless and stuck. Yet something within you knows there is more to your life than this cold dark morning, more than this frozen lake–and more to you than no reflection.

You bend closer to the lake's surface. Un-gloving a hand, your fingertips brush crusts of miniscule frost crystals. The ice beneath is tough. You could easily stride to the far side. Through many dark nights and endless winters you have learned to navigate this frozen lake knowing where the ice is thickest; where it is thinner and weaker close to the edges; where, if it were to crack, you could drown in deep crevices of underwater boulders or become entangled in weeds. Yet, as particles of ice-frost melt on blood-warm fingers, weariness overwhelms you. You are tired of being skilled at navigating your way through the darkness, being frozen and invisible. A yearning is stirring. More than that–a knowing is calling you from beyond the trees through the still night sky. You know it is time for the darkness to lift over spring and the high noon sun to thaw the ice, melt the snow and provide the clear light where you can see, in the turquoise blue surface of the lake, the crisp vision of who you truly are. Who you were born to be. It's time.

Tell me, for what is it that your heart yearns?

....

....

....

....

....

....

....

....

....

....

....

Are you ready?

Welcome To The Shift Café!

I'm excited you've made the decision to embark on a life changing journey. In this introduction, you'll discover:

- How to work with each chapter (I call them *Sips*).
- The resources you'll require.
- How much time each *Sip* will take to read and complete.

Vital Vision

You'll also get to take part in your first Shift Café activities that are designed to help you work out what your heart desires and how to attain it. This is called your Vital Vision. First, however, let me tell you a little about me and why I'm so passionate about helping you.

About Cindy

I recently turned 70. In the year preceding this, I became deeply depressed. Feeling old, many aspects of my life had lost their sparkle. I was frightened that my vibrant, adventuresome and fulfilling life was over. Does this resonate with you? I knew it was time for me to take stock of my life and make some shifts. Within the next year, I had:

- Changed many aspects of my social circle.
- Joined a new church.
- Began painting.
- Become a political activist.
- Commenced writing my first book.

Of course, this didn't happen overnight. I needed to take quality time to reflect on my life in order to work out what needed to change. My favorite time for this was while sitting at my living room table with a hot coffee, overlooking the trees in my garden — and the fields beyond. Often, my beloved dog Bailey would sit by my heels. I came to think of this space as *The Shift Café*.

```
┌─────────────────────────────────────────────────┐
│                 The Shift Café                    │
│              ⌒⋇⌒⋇⌒⋇⌒                             │
│  A serene space for quality time & gentle reflection so that you can │
│                    work out:                      │
│                                                   │
│   •   What shifts you need to improve in your life. │
│   •   How to attain these.                        │
└─────────────────────────────────────────────────┘
```

Breakthrough

I was lucky. I knew how to help myself as I've spent the better part of my adult life working on each next big breakthrough.

```
┌─────────────────────────────────────────────────┐
│        The Shift Café Definition of Breakthrough   │
│              ⌒⋇⌒⋇⌒⋇⌒                             │
│        An instance of achieving a vital insight that creates │
│           solutions to a situation that feels stuck. │
└─────────────────────────────────────────────────┘
```

It seems like we're always working hard to level up or just get more. The problem with this is that most things we try aren't really designed to help us get an actual breakthrough. Throughout my career, I've been determined to help people create genuine breakthroughs in both personal and business life — joy enhancing shifts that lead to more time, money and freedom. Not to mention enhanced self-esteem.

```
┌─────────────────────────────────────────────────┐
│            The Shift Café Definition of Shift     │
│              ⌒⋇⌒⋇⌒⋇⌒                             │
│         A conscious movement away from disappointing │
│      aspects of your life so that you can welcome in life enhancing │
│    experiences and feelings that truly serve your highest well-being. │
└─────────────────────────────────────────────────┘
```

The Shift Café — A Space for Creative Solutions

In *The Shift Café*, I share with you the creative techniques that I've developed and used with hundreds of corporate colleagues and private clients. These are the same tools that have them reporting back to me with comments such as:

- *Cindy, I finally feel fulfilled in the work I'm doing. You helped me get out of a situation I hated and now I'm using my greatest strengths to not only succeed but also do something I absolutely love. Thank you!*
- *I was so tired of setting the same goals over and over and not getting anywhere. Thank you for helping me shift. It feels great to achieve so much in such a short time.*
- *Your plan has helped me get much more done in a day. I am no longer working late at night or on the weekends. My family and I are grateful.*

Every time I see comments like this, I want to jump for joy. I love being able to share my expertise and then hear about the life-changing shifts my clients are getting as a result. I want you to have that same experience.

The Shift Café Journey

Taking you on an imaginary nature walk through The Shift Café garden, you'll undertake simple, bite-sized creative activities. Each activity will bring your Vital Vision to life. Each task acts as a stepping-stone that will help:

- Decide your next, most life enhancing, shift and breakthrough.
- Create an action plan to attain it with ease — and fun!
- Identify any limiting beliefs and obstacles that might be holding you back.
- Work out effective ways to release both of these.

Resources

To help you with these activities, you will need:

- A dedicated paper journal or file on your computer.
- Pens and/or pencils.
- A creatively inspiring workspace — your own Shift Café!

Reading Time

- The whole book can be read in less than five hours.
- Each *Sip* can be read in less than twenty minutes.

Create Your Own Shift Cafe Contemplation Nook

The Shift Café Definition of Contemplation Nook

Your own private Shift Café haven within your
home or garden.

Many readers and workshop attendees enjoy creating their own private Shift Café haven within their home or garden. Closets and storage rooms have been de-cluttered, cleaned up and transformed into serene sanctuaries complete with table, chairs and journals for quality time and self-reflection. One of my attendees referred to this as her Shift Café Contemplation Nook. We liked it so much that it stuck! Why not allocate an area in your home to become your Shift Café Contemplation Nook? In the space below, make notes on where your Contemplation Nook will be and why.

My Contemplation Nook will be....

Coffee Time!

The Shift Café Definition of Coffee Time

A period of quality time within each *Sip* devoted to
guided activities that will bring your Vital Vision to life.

Guided Activities

Each activity can be completed in less than thirty minutes and is designed to
fit neatly into your personal and professional life. However, many people find
them so enriching that they choose to take longer. You may love to devour
each task in one sitting or spread them over several days or even a whole
week. The deeper you engage, the more value you'll receive.

Who is The Shift Café for?

The Shift Café journey is for you if you're at stage in life where you're wondering:

Now what?

Who am I now?

How do I want to live my life?

When clients first work with me, they often share how they feel as if:

- They no longer have value in society.
- Life has passed them by before they attained their dreams.
- It's too late to change their lifestyle and habits.
- They're no longer worthy of exciting adventures or a joyful existence.

Many talk of feeling hopeless. Some feel this as they become empty nesters. Others plummet emotionally following the loss of a job or the end of a successful career. More still experience a sense of lost-identity following late-in-life divorces or widowhood. Does this resonate with you? What, if anything, is causing you to feel hopeless?

Listen to Your Heart

We experience these difficult emotions and beliefs in many ways — sometimes as low moods or as ripples of anxiety fluttering through our bodies. We also feel these emotions in our hearts. In *The Shift Café*, we focus mainly on your heart. We believe a conscious connection with your heart aids authentic high-level shifts.

Are You Tired of Feeling This Way?

You are? Great! You're in the right place! You'll get the most out of this journey if you're ready to shake off these despondent feelings and step into the most passionate and joyful expression of yourself — no matter your age. In fact, **you refuse to let age be a barrier to joy.**

Is this Journey for You?

Combining decades of professional and personal experience, I'm on a mission to empower determined and passionate people, like you, to reach your full potential.
I promise to help you:

- Identify your unique gifts.
- Create the courage to honor them.
- Detect and resolve obstacles that hinder your progress.

- Develop a life strategy where you feel joyfully content.
- Celebrate your successes – and share them with the world!

These SHIFTs begin with YOU! You're now ready to enjoy your first Coffee Time! Grab your drink and journal. Make yourself comfortable. Let's begin.

Coffee Time!

Activity 1–Heart Connection
Let's practice connecting with your heart.
Close your eyes. Place your hands over your heart. Breathe in.

Tell me, how does your heart currently feel?

....

....

....

....

....

....

....

....

....

Tell me, when was the last time you gave your heart this level of quality time?

....

....

....

....

....

....

....

....

....

Tell me, how did it feel to connect with your heart?

....

....

....

....

....

....

....

....

Activity 2 – The Level 10 Exercise.

One of the things that influences how our day, and life, goes is our effort level and attitude. I want to share one of my favorite exercises that I learned from my good friend and sales coach, Eric Lofholm. It's called the **Level 10 exercise.** You can simply read how it works or you can play along with me. Have your journal in hand and make detailed notes in response to each of the questions below. Let's begin.

Imagine you have ten energy levels with one being the lowest and ten being the highest amount of energy and enthusiasm. Imagine that I'm saying, 'good morning' to you. I want you to say 'good morning' back to me at a level 6 in terms of energy & enthusiasm.

Let's say you just did that. **How did that feel?**

Now we're going to try it again and this time we're going to play at a level 8, adding in a little more energy and enthusiasm. If you want to smile this time, you have my permission to smile. Let's give it a try — here we go, 'good morning!'

How did that feel?

Let's try it one last time. I want you to give it everything you've got. Let's try a **Level 10** 'good morning'.

How did that feel?

The first time we did it, whether you played along, or just read, it was a level 6. The last time, a Level 10, you hopefully noticed that you felt a positive shift in your energy levels. I have another question for you. As you've approached all aspects of your life on a daily basis over the last 30 days, at what level have you been playing? My belief is that you get out of life what you put into it and all the rewards are for those who play full out. Yet who decides what level we play at on a daily basis? That's right — we do. Here's a question for you: *today, at what level are you committed to play?* I want you to make the decision right now that you're going to give your life everything you've got. Then I want you to ask yourself: *at what level am I committed to play* as I work through *The Shift Café* activities? Don't worry if Level 10 feels too much for you right now. It's okay to commit to the Level that currently feels right for you.

Tell me, what level currently feels right for you?

....

Make Your Commitment!

Creating a contract with yourself can help you stay true to your goals. Why not sign the contract below?

The Shift Café Contract

I am committed to listening to my heart and playing at my best possible level as I journey through the activities in *The Shift Café*.

Signed .... **Date** ....

Tell me, how will you know if you're playing at that level — what will you be doing?

....

....

....

Congratulations! You've definitely earned your coffee!
In today's *Sip*, you have:

- Clarified the definition of a breakthrough.
- Clarified the definition of shift.
- Decided that you're committed to making massive shifts in your life.
- Connected with your heart, nature and *The Shift Café*.
- Committed to playing at Level 10 every single day of your magnificent life!

In the next *Sip*, I invite you to: ***Tell Me,*** Who Inspires You? See you there!

The Shift Café
Nurturing your wisdom, intelligence, beauty and spirit — one sip at a time.

SONG OF AWAKENING

by Jamie Cloud

All quiet in the winter dark,
the echo of a fox's bark,
a lonesome howl as wild things prowl
amid the oak trees cold and stark.

But look, a pale light rising swift
through violet clouds that calmly drift
as if in prayer on the frosty air,
awaiting dawn's enchanting gift!

So take heart, wild things, take heart!
For seasons come and go,
and when it's time for flowers to grow
the winter must depart.

Be still then, child, and do not fight;
bid farewell to the fading night.
When all is done come greet the sun
that fills these woods again with light.
Yes, all is done, come greet the sun
That fills your waking soul with light.

Yes, all is done, come greet the sun
That fills your waking soul with light.

Contemplation Nook

Sip 2

Nurturing Inspiration

Progress is not achieved by luck or accident, but by working on yourself.
Epictetus

The Shift Café Definition of Inspiration

To be stimulated and motivated to create life
enhancing shifts by the creativity and wisdom
of others — and your own heart's desires.

Early Morning

It is not yet dawn. I woke early, much earlier than is customary. At heart, I'm a night owl. I brew my coffee with faithful Bailey at my heels then draw my Shift Café table and journal closer to the window. I want to see the stars and winter moon that gleam behind silhouettes of hickory trees. Opening my journal, I feel grateful for the beauty in this scene. As my eyes grow used to the low light, I sketch the shadows dancing through branches as my heart opens to the day. Thoughts and feelings flow until one word rises and settles:

Inspiration

My heart wonders further until memories are recalled of loved ones who've inspired and profoundly influenced my life. I want to speak with you of them and also ask you:

Tell Me, Who Inspires You?

Tell Me, Who Inspires You?

> ### INTENTIONS
>
>
>
> 1. To identify who has been a major positive influence on your life.
> 2. To clarify how their legacy has enhanced your life.
> 3. To identify your own unique gifts that you can gift as a legacy to others.
> 4. To understand how this can help you create powerful shifts in your life – for yourself personally, those you love and beyond.

In *Sip 1*, you:

- Clarified the definition of shift and breakthrough.
- Decided that you are committed to making gentle and powerful shifts in your life.
- Connected with your heart, nature & created your personal Shift Café.
- Committed to listening to your heart & playing at your best level every single day of your magnificent life!

Breakthrough

An instance of achieving a vital insight that creates solutions to a situation that feels stuck.

Tell me, at what level did you honor your heart this week?

1   2   3   4   5   6   7   8   9   10

What worked for you? Why?
What didn't work for you? Why not?
What do you still need to do?

To Shift

Welcoming life enhancing experiences that serve your highest well-being.

....

....

....

Inspiration & Legacy

In today's *Sip*, you're going to explore who has had a major positive impact on your life. It can be helpful to look back at the influences of the past in order to support your present and determine your future. Additionally, you'll examine how and why they've been an influence, asking: *what legacy did they gift to me?*

Legacy

The common understanding of legacy is *something that we leave to people to receive after we die*, but here's how I see legacy: imagine you *live your life to the very fullest*, however you define that. I encourage you to examine legacy while you're still alive. *What can you gift to others so that they can achieve? For what will they remember you?*

The Shift Café Definition of Legacy

- What can you gift to others so that they can achieve?
- For what will they remember you?

At this point, you may feel that you have nothing to offer others or that you will leave nothing by which to be remembered. Everyone, however, has something of value to share. Take a few moments to dig deep. Think of your kind act to a neighbor, a time when you helped a friend or encouraged a member of your family when they were fearful.

The Shift Café Legacy Seeds

These acts of kindness, care and thoughtfulness are the things by which you will be remembered. I call these types of acts The Shift Café Legacy Seeds.

The Shift Café Definition of Legacy Seeds

Positive deeds we do, with love, for others
who will remember us for these acts.
In their turn, they'll pass them on to others.

Inspirational Women

I've been fortunate enough to be supported by several generations of strong women including, as you can see in this old family picture, my mother, grandmother and great-grandmother. However, it was my great-aunt Florence who came to have a major impact on my life.

Great-Aunt Florence — My Heroine

Following her death, and in the ensuing years, I've come to realize the major

life enhancing impact on many of my actions, feelings and beliefs that she imparted on me during my childhood. I've even seen her influence continue with my own son, Brandon. At the time, however, I wasn't sufficiently mature to fully understand the value of the impact of her life on mine. Part of me now wishes

I could go back and live my time with her again only, this time, with greater appreciation and acknowledgment. Unable to do that, I asked myself: *what are the lessons I've learned from her?* What legacy did she give me — not after she died but while she was alive?

I recalled how she had friends of all ages. It was the same with my mother. In my early twenties, when I heard my mother speaking of her friends at work who were my age, I wondered: why would they want to be friends with an old person like my mom? Now, being fortunate enough to also have friends of all ages, I fully understand, value and celebrate the many gifts these friendships bring to my life. Both my great-aunt Florence and mother knew the value of living with an inquisitive mind, open heart and broad perspective.

Bailey nudges me, prompting me to rise and take him to the garden. As he frolics in freshly fallen snow, I marvel at the bright light of the moon. In the silence, further memories rise: my mother's smile; Aunt Florence's laugh; the gentle touch of both their hands …

Following my first realization about Great-Aunt Florence, I came to see how her many positive qualities became lifelong legacy influences on my own life. To this day, I'm proud to continue her legacy within every one of my vital life decisions. To remember and remain loyal to her values, I created a list: *How to Live a Legacy Legendary Life, Great-Aunt Florence Style*. Take a moment to read the list I created. I wonder what you'll think of Great-Aunt Florence!?

How to Live a Legacy Legendary Life, Great-Aunt Florence Style

1: Be open-minded.

Aunt Florence listened consistently to the current affairs programs on her radio and TV so that she was always able to engage visitors in diverse conversations. She excelled at being inquisitive, reflective and non-judgmental, always willing to hear a range of perspectives on all subjects.

2: Have friends of all ages.

Even in her later years, Aunt Florence socialized and entertained friends of all ages. They loved her company and lively discussions.

3: Keep Learning.

When she was homebound during winter months, Aunt Florence would teach herself a new skill. I recall her learning the countries in Africa and their capital cities and all of the presidents and vice-presidents of the USA.

4: Create, and write down, fun and heart-centered goals.

Another winter activity was to draw a plan of her beloved vegetable patch so that when spring arrived she was prepared for planting.

5: Celebrate.

Aunt Florence loved to decorate her home to celebrate all the holidays. Also, when anyone in the family succeeded at something new, she was the first to offer congratulations.

6: Share — sometimes anonymously.

As a huge benefactor in her local town, she preferred to support her favorite causes anonymously, never feeling the need to brag or gloat.

7: Surprise People.

Always young at heart, she loved to play games and create fun surprises for people. When my son Brandon was little, he loved her butterscotch pies. On visits, he would eagerly ask if she had made butterscotch pie. Pretending she hadn't, she would then take Brandon on a hunt around the house until they found the pie in some obscure place. The fun attached to the pie made it taste even sweeter!

8: Cherish Nature.

Aunt Florence lived simply, taking pleasure in her surrounding landscape. She especially loved all flowers, especially peonies, tulips and daffodils — the perennials that came up each year.

9: Stay True to Yourself.

If I had to use one word to define how Aunt Florence lived her life, it would be authentic.

The Shift Café Definition of Authentic

The courage to live a life true to your own needs and desires regardless of what others may think, say or do.

Each year, Aunt Florence visited the annual Indiana State Fair with her friends. While they eagerly visited exhibitions of quilts and cakes, Aunt Florence loved to visit the livestock pens even though it wasn't traditional for women to take an interest in such things. She used to tell me, 'all of these old women wanted to go and look at the pies but I went to the livestock barns because they were castrating the pigs and I remember my father doing that when I was a child.' Relishing the smells and sounds, she delighted in recalling happy childhood memories growing up on a farm. I admire how she never shied away from making, and taking action on, empowered and independent decisions that honored her deepest desires, creating immense personal happiness. Authentic living at its finest.

10: Enjoy life to the fullest.

All of the activities on this list certainly convey how Aunt Florence lived life to her fullest potential. However, it wasn't all smooth sailing for her. Like many people, including you I'm sure, she had to find the courage to face many difficult situations. This included the stigma of leaving and divorcing a violent and much older husband with whom she had run across the state line at the age of fifteen to marry. After that difficult time, she always strived to live a Level 10 life.

Coffee Time!

I'm sure you can see why Aunt Florence's life had a huge influence on mine. It's time to identify your Shift Café inspirational hero/ine! Pour your coffee. Gather your journal. Let's begin.

The Shift Café Definition of Inspirational Hero/ine

A person who lives their lives in a way that inspires others to be more intentional in their own life.

Imagine yourself standing under the winter moon. Close your eyes. Feel the cool air on your face.

Tell me, how is your heart today?

....

....

....

Tell me, what does legacy mean to you?

....

....

....

Feel the moon's energy connecting with the energy within your own body.

Tell me, which inspirational person has helped to gift that energy to your soul?

....

....

....

If you find this task difficult, use the following guidelines:

HELP! I have lots of people who spring to mind, how do I choose?

Make a list of all these people in your journal. Listen to which person your gut instinct guides you towards. Write their name boldly on a fresh page in your journal. If selecting one person from your list doesn't come easily to mind, make notes on all of the ways in which each person has positively impacted your life. Once it's clear who has influenced you in the most ways, write their name boldly on a fresh page in your journal.

HELP! I'm stuck. I can't think of anyone. What should I do?

Perhaps you can't remember anyone, or only people who've had a negative impact. Perhaps you can only think of someone who had a few positive traits but were inconsistent. Make a list of all the people who come to mind. Don't filter, judge or edit. Keep going until someone appears on your list that brings a happy memory to you. Even if it's just one happy memory, that's good enough. Write that person's name boldly on a fresh page in your journal.

HELP! My inspirational person isn't a real person. Is this okay?

As you continue with the activity, you might find that other people who trigger happier memories may come to mind. Swap them in for your first person. These may include friends, neighbors, relatives or even a stranger who was once kind to you. You might even discover that your inspirational person isn't real. Perhaps they're a character from a book or even a video game. This is okay. However, be assured, one person or character relating to one happy memory is sufficient to help you complete this task.

Now that you've identified your Shift Café inspirational hero/ine,

Tell me, how did they inspire and influence you?

1.

2.

3.

Tell me, how did this enhance your life?

....

....

....

....

....

....

....

Tell me, what additional gifts do you have?

....

....

....

....

....

....

....

....

Tell me, which of your gifts do you wish to gift to others so that they can achieve?

....

....

....

....

....

....

....

....

....

The Shift Café Sketching Corner

Draw a picture of the moon in a winter sky. Decorate it with the gifts you want to radiate to others.

Tell me, how does this make your heart feel?

Nurturing Inspiration – Vital Vision Shift Action Step

Inspiration

To be stimulated and motivated to create life enhancing shifts by the creativity and wisdom of others – and your own heart's desires.

With each new *Sip*, you'll be invited to identify and commit to taking one **Shift Action Step**.

The Shift Café Definition of Shift Action Step

Each **Shift Action Step** is an action, thought or feeling that will bring you closer to accomplishing your heart's yearning.

Tell me, what *Inspiration and Legacy* focused Shift Action Step will you take this week?

The Shift Café Legacy Seeds

....

....

....

Positive deeds we do, with love, for others who will remember us for these acts.

Tell me, at what level are you going to honor your *Inspiration and Legacy* focused Shift Action Step this week?

1   2   3   4   5   6   7   8   9   10

Tell me, how will you know that you are honoring them effectively?

....

....

....

Congratulations! In this *Sip* you have:

- Identified who has been a major positive influence on your life.
- Clarified how their legacy has enhanced your life.
- Identified your own unique gifts that you can gift as a legacy for others.
- Understood how this can help you create powerful shifts in your life — for yourself personally, those you love and beyond.

Remember:

> *The moon is over 4 billion years old and still it shines.*
> *How long do you want your light to continue shining?*

With your next *Shift Café Sip*, you'll connect with your heart's deepest desires as I ask you to: **Tell Me**, What is Your Vital Vision? I look forward to seeing you there!

My Legacy

by Christy Dance-Greenhut

My gift to the world, my legacy,
It's a constant, ever changing, part of me.
I won't leave a statue or a portrait in the museum of art,
Instead I hope to leave a thousand pieces of my heart.
I hope those I love still hear me saying, I Believe in You,
And that it gives them the courage to make their dreams come true.
I hope I'm that whisper, perhaps even a calming voice,
That helps them find peace when they have to make a difficult choice.
I hope I've set the example to show kindness to all,
And shared with them my struggles, even after a fall.
I hope they've seen me rise and find a different way,
To start again, to find the hope and the beauty of each new day.
I can't claim these values simply as mine alone,
I was gifted along the way with the angels I have known.
I have borrowed parts of their legacy to pass along to you,
And I hope that I have left you something that you can borrow too.

Contemplation Nook

Sip 3
Nurturing Your Dreams

Hold on to your true aspirations no matter what is going on around you.
Epictetus

The Shift Café Definition of Dream

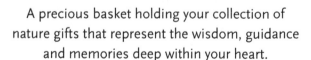

An unfulfilled desire that your heart yearns to bring to life.

Serenity Basket

The Shift Café Definition of Serenity Basket

A precious basket holding your collection of
nature gifts that represent the wisdom, guidance
and memories deep within your heart.

A chill wind whips through the trees sparking flurries of snow into the air. Undeterred, Bailey snuffles into the roots of my favorite trees; pines and hickories. Tall with tufts of flaky bark, hickory trees never fail to make me feel strong and connected to something bigger than myself — Mother Nature in all her glory.

Knowing that I will not return to sleep, I decide to gather foliage and pine cones to decorate my home for the Thanksgiving celebrations that will soon be with us.

Collecting my Serenity Basket, I walk towards the hill that lies beyond the bottom of my garden. Picking my way carefully through roots and shrubs, the smooth wicker of the basket between my fingers recalls memories of similar baskets once used by both my aunt Florence and grandmother. My grandmother used hers to collect vegetables and flowers from her garden while Aunt Florence filled hers with eggs from her chicken coop.

I can't remember when I first acquired mine but it has fared well over the years. In spring I use it to forage for edible mushrooms. In fall it overflows with apples and juicy berries. Today, of course, few fruits are here for the picking but I delight in the fresh smells of the pine cones and foliage that soon fill my basket. I think of Aunt Florence's many wonderful achievements throughout her life and all that she gave to others yet find myself wondering if she fulfilled all her dreams. In our Sip today, I invite you to consider your dreams, asking:

Tell Me, What is Your One Vital Vision?

Tell Me, What is Your ONE Vital Vision?

In the last *Sip* you:

- Identified who has been a major positive influence on your life.
- Clarified how their legacy has enhanced your life.
- Identified your own unique gifts that you can gift as a legacy to others.
- Understood how this can help you create powerful shifts in your life — for yourself, those you love and beyond.

Legacy

What you gift to others so that they can achieve.

Tell me, at what level did you honor your heart and *Inspiration and Legacy* focused Shift Action Step this week?

1   2   3   4   5   6   7   8   9   10

What will they remember you for?

What worked for you? Why?
What didn't work for you? Why not?
What do you still need to do?

....

....

....

Remember, there's no right or wrong. It's simply helpful to be aware of what level you're living at. If you struggled with any area, it might be helpful to journal on why you found it difficult. Creating life-enhancing shifts requires constant reflection and self-awareness. Equally, it's important to recognize what went well. Be sure to celebrate this and understand why things flowed for you so that you can repeat this success.

In this *Sip*, you're going to:

Vital Vision

A dream that your heart yearns to attain.

- Clarify your top three most desired dreams and goals for the next year.
- Create your one Vital Vision for the next twelve weeks.
- Commit to implementing your Shift Action Step.

The Shift Café Definition of Vital Vision

A clear picture of how your unfulfilled dream
will look and feel once it's been attained.

To help Shift Café workshops participants clarify their Vital Vision, I ask them: 'Tell me, what do you want to do or be when you grow up?' Clarifying your vision will help you identify the precise shifts you'll need to commit to in order to bring it to life.

Bailey barks. Ahead of us, we see a shadow of a low and speedy animal. The long bushy tail of a fox swishes against the shadows and light of the dawning day. We'd clearly scared it. On it ran, over the open meadow through the thick snow until it reached the safety of a copse of trees on the far side of the field. I imagined its heart pounding in terror. Waiting, listening and hyper-alert, it would not know if we were about to inflict harm. Even in the sanctuary of its hiding place, it did not know if it was safe. It could only hope that the unfamiliar copse would provide sufficient protection.

Coffee Time!

From Comfort Zone into the Unknown

The Shift Café Definition of Comfort Zone

A feeling of psychological, emotional and physical safety.

As you step out of your comfort zone and into your Vital Vision, you may, like the fox, also feel fear. After all, you don't know if you're going to succeed or fail. Will others support, ridicule or hinder you? Fear and vulnerability may arise causing a feeling of overwhelm. As you'll know by now, here in *The Shift Café*, we don't let any of these things stop us! Taking one sip and Shift Action Step at a time, you'll be able to achieve things that you haven't yet dreamed. Grab your coffee!

Vital Vision Clarity Quiz — a Twelve-Week Plan

Tell me, how clear is your Vital Vision for the next twelve weeks?

From the descriptions below, circle the answer that accurately represents how you feel in relation to your current life visions, dreams and goals.

A: Crystal Clear

You know exactly what you wish to change in your life and how to accomplish this.

If this is you, I have a challenge for you. Are you willing to believe that you can develop this vision in ways you can't yet imagine, perhaps beyond your wildest dreams? I truly believe we have the capacity to expand beyond what we can consciously visualize. Are you open to exploring this idea?

B: Blurry

You have a vague idea of what you would like to attain but can't yet articulate it and feel unclear about how to accomplish this.

This can feel frustrating but it's also a good starting point. From this place of confusion we begin to weed out what is, and is not, working so that the shifts towards feeling fully alive become easier to attain.

C: Invisible?

You have no idea what it is you're seeking, you just know something isn't right and requires a shift.

This can feel despairing. However, for anyone beginning the journey of creating transformative shifts and breakthroughs, it's, potentially, the perfect starting point. I understand how you might find this hard to believe. After my son Ryan was stillborn at almost full-term, despair consumed my life. I had no idea how I was going to survive my grief or accept my loss. Something had to shift. All I could rely on was my trust in God. Maybe you're not religious however I encourage you to trust that, somehow, the support you need is on its way. You may not know what it is or how it will arrive for you — but it is there.

Lifting Bailey, determined to not let him add to the fox's fear, I walked gently by. I hoped the fox would find calm, trusting that we had left it in peace and would bring it no harm. I head towards the incline leading to the summit of Vital Vision Hill. How are you? Do you feel calmer now that you've taken this first step towards creating your Vital Vision? Perhaps you now feel more able to trust yourself.

Trust

Whichever answer you circled, trust that this is okay. Identifying your starting point is the first pivotal step towards attaining your desired shifts. It also means you're ready to take the next exciting step: becoming crystal clear about your Vital Vision.

Your Vital Vision — Identify Your Current Dreams and Goals

By the end of this section, you'll have ascertained your one Vital Vision to work on during the next twelve weeks. However, to help you reach this point, you're going to think further ahead to this time next year. By knowing this, you'll become clearer on the steps you need to take in the short term to help you arrive there.

Tell me, by this time next year, what dreams and goals would you like to have accomplished, if nothing were out of reach? What will you be able to do differently? Don't think too hard. What's the first thing that comes to mind? Feel free to list as many ideas as possible. Make detailed notes in your journal.

HELP! If you're finding it difficult to imagine your dreams and goals, take a few moments to journal the following questions.

By this time next year:

- Who do I want to become?
- What do I want to be doing/feeling?
- How do I want to be/feel?
- Where do I want to be doing this?
- Why do I want to be doing this?
- When do I want to be doing this

Top Three Dreams and Goals
Once you've completed your list, I'd like you to identify your top three dreams and goals. Write them in your journal or record them:

1.

2.

3.

Arriving at the summit of Vital Vision Hill, the night gives way to shafts of deep-blue light, brightening the darkness. My eyes are drawn forward — beyond the summit. Behind me is the direction from which I've traveled. Ahead is the vision of where I could potentially travel, My future. What would I see? What guidance and ideas could this view gift me? What, in the growing daylight, would I want to see? Imagine that you are also on the summit of Vital Vision Hill. What view of your future does it reveal?

Refine!

You've now identified your top three dreams and goals that you would like to have attained by this time next year. This will have helped you clarify important priorities in your life. Now, however, you're going to become super clear. Instead of thinking ahead twelve months, you're going to focus solely on the next twelve weeks so that you can stride towards your dreams and goals comfortably. To support this, you're now going to identify your ONE Vital Vision.

Vital Vision

From the three top dreams and goals that you've just identified, which one dream would you like to focus on for the next twelve weeks? This ONE dream now becomes your Shift Café Vital Vision. Write it clearly below.

The Vital Vision that I will attain over the next twelve weeks is:

....

....

....

The Shift Café Sketching Corner

Draw or collage a full color version of your Vital Vision.
Label and make notes. The more detailed you are, the more success
you're likely to achieve.

Place a copy of this picture and notes in your Serenity Basket.
You can review it regularly on your journey to help you remain focused
and clear.

Tell me, did you gain clarity? If so, what is your crystal-clear Vital Vision for the next twelve weeks?

....

....

....

....

....

....

....

....

....

....

....

....

....

....

....

....

....

....

....

Nurturing Dreams – Vital Vision Shift Action Step

Your Next Vital Vision Shift Action Step

Take a few moments to decide your one action, thought or feeling that you can implement easily over the coming week that will take you one step closer to attaining your Vital Vision.

Tell me, what is your *Vital Vision* focused Shift Action Step for this week?

Vital Vision

A clear picture of how your unfulfilled dream will look and feel once it's been attained.

....

....

....

Tell me, at what level are you going to honor this Shift Action Step in the coming week?

  1   2   3   4   5   6   7   8   9   10   *Trust yourself*

Tell me, how are you going to accomplish this?

....

....

....

Commitment

In your journal, write the following commitment statement and sign it.

I, (*insert your name*) , ...

commit to (*insert your Shift Action/Thought/Feeling*)

....

....

....

....

....

....

This will take me one step closer to attaining (*state your Vital Vision*)

....

....

....

....

....

....

Signature ....

Date ....

Congratulations! In this *Sip* you have:

- Explored a range of dreams and goals that you would like to attain over the next year.
- Clarified your top three most desired dreams and goals for the next year.
- Identified your **ONE** Vital Vision for the next twelve weeks.
- Identified the one Vital Vision Shift Action Step that you will implement this week to bring you closer to attaining your Vital Vision.
- Committed to implementing your Shift Action Step.

You've certainly earned your coffee this week! Relax, unwind and visualize yourself in The Shift Café at the end of the next twelve weeks. See yourself living the reality of your Vital Vision.

Remember:

> *You'll be able to achieve things that you've not yet dreamed.*

I look forward to seeing you in the *Contemplation Nook for Sip 4* where you'll be nurturing positivity as I ask you: **Tell Me,** For What Are You Grateful? See you there!

Even Now, After All This

by Teo Eve

palaces of frozen ice crumble,
their battlements break off the bergs
like softening snow.

the glaciers
between us
thaw.

Contemplation Nook

Sip 4
Nurturing Your Positivity

The happiness of your life depends upon the quality of your thoughts.

Marcus Aurelius

The Shift Café Definition of Positivity

Creating and maintaining an optimistic mindset when shifting through challenges as you attain your Vital Vision.

Gratitude Valley
Dawn

Trilling birds hail the new day as we carefully pick our way along the ridge away from Vital Vision summit. Taking care not to slip on protruding boulders, we head towards a wide ledge. Soft light from the remnants of the fading moon reveals a small hare. Even though it's unusual for such creatures to venture to high ground, I often see them here. Today, this one is nibbling tufts of grass poking through snow. I hold Bailey close, not wishing to scare or disturb. Intent on grazing, it hardly notices our presence. The ancient Greeks viewed the hare as an earthly vision of the Goddess Aphrodite — the Goddess of Love. Others saw her as symbolic of fertility, rebirth and resurrection. How fitting that she is appearing as you are on the cusp of transforming your life. The peacefulness in this scene calms my heart, filling it with gratitude for the simple things in life.

From this high ledge I turn, shifting my attention away from the view of the future we explored in the last Sip back to the view over the valley from where we first climbed. I see the farmland I grew up on, the location of the first school in which I ever taught. In the distance is the outline of the city where I gave birth to my son. The Shift Café table is set by the window of the living room in the home that I share with Tim, my beloved husband. On days when I feel nervous of what the future holds, I take time to gratefully cast my eye over this valley drawing strength and guidance from the many wonderful memories and experiences my life has, thus far, gifted me. As these have shaped who I am today, I like to think of this landscape as Gratitude Valley.

As you stand on this ledge with me, imagine that among the lake, cornfields and forest, you can also see the difficult and positive memories and experiences of your past that have shaped who you've become today. In today's Sip, you'll explore how gratitude for these experiences can help you attain your Vital Vision. I ask you:

Tell Me, For What Are You Grateful?

Tell Me, For What You Are Grateful?

INTENTIONS

To:
- Clarify The Shift Café meaning of gratitude.
- Explore your personal relationship with gratitude.
- Examine how this supports the successful attainment of your Vital Vision.

In the last *Sip*, you:

- Explored a range of dreams and goals that you would like to attain over the next year.
- Clarified your top three most desired dreams and goals for the next year.
- Identified your **ONE** Vital Vision for the next twelve weeks.
- Identified the **ONE** Vital Vision Shift Action Step that you would implement to bring you closer to attaining your overall Vital Vision.
- Committed to implementing your Shift Action Step.

Tell me, at what level did you honor your *Vital Vision* focused Shift Action Step this week?

1   2   3   4   5   6   7   8   9   10

What worked for you?   Why?

What didn't work for you?   Why not?

What do you still need to do?

....

....

....

Remember, there's no right or wrong.

Tell me, how did this help to support the overall development of your Vital Vision?

....

....

....

Creating My Vital Vision

When I was at the beginning of writing this book, I had only a vague idea of what I wanted to include. I could see hazy shapes, perhaps the outline of books on shelves or blurred figures of future readers. I could see myself standing on a platform delivering a speech that described the good I hoped *The Shift Café* would bring to my readers and workshop participants. Like you, I had created my Vital Vision:

To write a book to support people who feel lost, alone and helpless so that they discover the power in their potential thus enabling them to shift into their hidden dreams and create a life full of inspiration, celebration and joy.

Of course, I had no idea exactly what *The Shift Café* as a final book would look like. I didn't yet know each of my required Shift Action Steps to bring it to fruition. For this, I had to listen intently each day to my heart's guidance. I don't mind admitting that at the beginning, and at many points along the way, I felt nervous and fearful of failure. It was easy to sink into self-doubt. I had no clue how to create a book. And, truth be told, I'm not one to sit down and spend hours writing. Along with my strong desire, I also experienced confusion, fear and doubts:

What do you know about writing a book?
You haven't got a clue.
You're too old.
Who do you think you are to believe you can attain this dream?

Does negative self-talk resonate with you?

When I find myself in these furrows of doubt, I find it helps to connect with positive emotions to help me shift into a more confident mindset. I believe the most important of these is gratitude. Once connected with the feelings and memories from the past for which I'm grateful, I immediately find it easier for my heart to connect with the wise guidance required to step through the fear and doubt of today's new dreams.

Gratitude – A Human Strength

The Shift Café Definition of Gratitude

A feeling in your heart that informs you that you've been engaged in an experience that has nourished and enhanced your sense of well-being and wisdom — and, often, the well-being and wisdom of others.

Skepticism

Sometimes, my workshop participants initially feel skeptical about gratitude. Some wonder if they can even remember an experience filled with such an emotion. They also question how it could help the attainment of their Vital Vision. I understand that when you're feeling dissatisfied with some aspects of life, or if life has treated you harshly, gratitude can be hard to feel.

Breast Cancer Diagnosis — Shifting from *Poor Me* to Gratitude

At the age of 56, I was diagnosed with breast cancer. The hospital had missed it for four years. Following a lumpectomy, I awaited a call from my doctor to see if they had the clear margins required to declare me cancer free. Unfortunately, this wasn't the case. The doctor gently informed me, 'we're going to have to operate again.' I fell into a deep depression. At a later appointment, after having received the all-clear, I was asked, 'how are you feeling?' Despite it making no sense, I explained that I still felt depressed. For my own mental and emotional well-being, I desperately needed to find a positive in my experience. To help me, I was invited to meet with an oncologist. She asked me to join a three-year clinical trial that would enable researchers to examine the relationship between breast cancer, DNA and medication. The results would help to determine the specific medication required for each individual breast cancer patient. Instantly, I realized how thousands of women in the future could benefit from my experience, treatment and trial participation. Just thinking about this shifted my mood and poor me attitude. I signed up and instantly felt grateful that from my own devastating experience, I had found a way to help others.

Gratitude — A Vital Foundation Stone.

I'm sure the hare on the ledge overlooking Gratitude Valley, like many other creatures in winter, wake up to snowy days and fear they may not find the sustenance they need for basic survival. Imagine how grateful they are when a nourishing blade of grass protrudes enough for them to fill themselves. Despite how fearful you may currently feel, or what difficulties you've experienced, I want you to know that there are good things in your life. You don't have to stay stuck. In fact, not only do I want you to identify the positives of your life, I also want you to build on them. The first vital foundation stone to support this is gratitude. Let's explore how gratitude can help you.

Coffee Time!

Connect with Your Heart

Take yourself for a real or imaginary walk in nature that nourishes you. Imagine yourself walking along the Vital Vision ridge to the ledge overlooking Gratitude Valley. Pay grateful attention to your whole body, including bones, muscles and tendons that work hard to support you. Next, thank your kidneys and liver for the silent work they undertake day and night to keep you well. Now, rest a moment and bring your hands to your heart.

Tell me, for what is your heart grateful today?

....

....

....

....

If you find this hard, work through the exercise below. Think of your current environment in *The Shift Café* landscape. Bring your attention to your whole life, including your home, family and work.

What is the one thing, in your entire life, for which you are most grateful?

To help you connect more deeply with gratitude, it's helpful to think of the one thing in your entire life for *which you are most grateful.*

Be as specific as you can. Use the questions below to help you.

- How old were you?
- Where were you?
- Who were you with?
- What were you doing?
- What were you wearing?
- What season was it?
- What could you hear, see, smell, taste, touch?
- What colors can you remember?
- What was said?

How Did You Feel?

This activity helps you to identify how gratitude feels personally to you. You'll feel these emotions in your body and heart. Below is a table of feelings to help you. **Circle** those that resonate with you.

Connected	Stimulated	Liked
Intimate	Adventurous	Sexy
Alive	Supported	Valued
Visible	Inspired	Responsible
Relaxed	Refreshed	Humble
Playful	Happy	Proud
Serious	Loved	Valid
Humorous	Curious	Intelligent
Joyful	Privileged	Youthful
Excited	Honored	Mature

Tell me, what personal feelings can you add to this list?

....

....

....

....

....

....

....

Using your above answer, write one paragraph to explain how you feel when you are grateful.

....

....

....

....

....

....

....

....

....

The Shift Café Sketching Corner

Gratitude Valley

Using the ideas from the above exercises, draw your own version of Gratitude Valley. What memories or experiences would you place there?

Label and make notes.

Place a copy of this picture and notes in your Serenity Basket.
You can review it regularly on your journey to
help you remain focused and clear.

Nurturing Positivity – Vital Vision Shift Action Step

Positivity

Creating and maintaining an optimistic mindset when shifting through challenges as you attain your Vital Vision.

The Shift Café Definition of Gratitude Journal

～ჯ～ჯ～ჯ～ჯ～ჯ～

A written list of everything, from the smallest to the largest, for which you feel gratitude throughout the day.

Gratitude Journal

For the next week, make a **Level 10** commitment to keeping a daily gratitude journal. Note everything from the smallest to largest things for which you feel grateful throughout the day. This will provide a daily reminder of the many wonderful aspects of your life. Make a note of how your feelings and life changes as a result of undertaking this exercise. By the way, it needn't take very long, around five minutes — the time it takes to heat the water for your coffee! Place this gratitude journal into your Serenity Basket. You can add to it throughout your journey with *The Shift Café* as you bring your Vital Vision to life. Additionally, it will provide a comforting reminder and support on days when gratitude is hard to feel.

Practice Gratitude

Take your newly found feeling of gratitude and make a pledge to show extra gratitude to someone you meet today. This could be a spouse, child, or friend. It could also be the checkout person at the grocery store, server at a restaurant or stranger in the street. Repeat on a daily basis.

Tell me, how does being generous with gratitude make you feel?

....

....

....

Tell me, what is one *Gratitude* focused Vital Vision Shift Action Step you can implement this week?

....

....

....

Tell me, how will this support the successful attainment of your Vital Vision?

....

....

....

Serenity Basket Heart Wisdom

The Shift Café Definition of Heart Wisdom

The hidden truth held deep in your heart.
*Listening to the whispers in your heart will guide you
to your Vital Vision.*

Serenity Basket Heart Wisdom

Reflect on this question:

From what I've learned today, does my heart have any further wisdom that will help me to attain my Vital Vision?

....

....

....

Place this guidance into your Serenity Basket. Let it help you on your journey through *The Shift Café*.

Bailey and I leave the hare, which has now been joined by several others. It is time to return home. My heart is full.

Congratulations! In this *Sip*, you have:

- Clarified *The Shift Café* meaning of gratitude.
- Explored your personal relationship with gratitude.
- Examined how this supports the successful attainment of your Vital Vision.

Remember:
> *There are good things in your life. You don't have to stay stuck. A vital foundation stone to shifting and feelings of being stuck is gratitude.*

With your next *Sip*, I ask you, **Tell Me**, What Does Success Mean to You? See you there!

BIRDSONG

by Andrew Roberts

I sat in my garden.
At least, I thought it was my
garden until many
birds landed nearby
singing in purest
synchronicity.
My heart beat to their rhythm.
We sang together.
I realised:
It was I who sat in their garden.
I felt privileged
to do so.

Contemplation Nook

Sip 5
Nurturing Success

Our greatest glory is not in never falling, but in rising each time we fall.
Confucius

The Shift Café Definition of Success

The attainment of your Vital Vision to
a level that feels rewarding.

Leaving the ledge and the hares, Bailey and I descend from Vital Vision Hill into Gratitude Valley. Taking an alternative route home from that of our ascent, we pass by fields where the corn has been picked. In the spring, corn seeds will again germinate deep in the earth. Now though, through shallower patches of snow, fall leaves from oaks and birches rooted along each edge of the fields protrude. Their golden hues mirror the early morning sun shimmering through low branches. Taking the track that runs through spruce trees, I gather small branches abundant with pine needles and place them in my Serenity Basket beside the pine cones. Soon I will use them to form a bough of welcome over my front door for guests attending my upcoming Thanksgiving celebrations.

Vital Vision lake is close by, to my left. Two swans have melted a hole through the layers of snow and ice covering the frozen surface. One washes itself, stretching its long neck and arching its wings. Occasionally, it raises itself almost out of the water as if to take flight before sinking once more into a preening of feathers. Its mate sleeps close by, head tucked under its wing. I feel grateful for this connection with nature at this, for me, unusual time of day.

Full daylight fills the sky as I re-enter my garden. Relieved to be home, Bailey leaps from my arms and bounds indoors. Plumes of smoke from the chimney tell me that Tim has lit our fire to welcome us. Once indoors, I relish the warmth as I remove my boots and head to the kitchen. Pouring myself a fresh cup of coffee, I return to my Shift Café table where my heart feels nourished by the soothing flicker of the fire's flames. Bailey snuggles at my feet, one paw resting against the Serenity Basket. I prepare for today's Sip in which I ask:

Tell Me, how do you define success?

Tell Me, How Do You Define Success?

INTENTION

~~~~~~~~~~~~~~~~~~

To create your personal definition for success
in relation to your Vital Vision.

In the last *Sip*, you:

- Clarified The Shift Café definition of gratitude.
- Explored your personal relationship with gratitude.
- Examined how gratitude supports the successful attainment of your Vital Vision.

Gratitude

A feeling in your heart that informs you that you've been engaged in an experience that has nourished your sense of well-being..

Tell me, at what level did you honor your *Gratitude* focused Shift Action Step this week?

<div align="center">

1   2   3   4   5   6   7   8   9   10

What worked for you?   Why?
What didn't work for you?   Why not?
What do you still need to do?

</div>

....

....

....

Tell me, how does this make your heart feel?

....

....

....

Defining Success

In order to attain any goal in life, including your Vital Vision, it's helpful to know exactly how you define success. This ensures that you have a clear picture of what you wish to achieve and will know when it's been attained. Each of us has a personal understanding of success. You may feel that, at this moment, your understanding of success is not crystal clear. Creating your personal definition of success specifically in relation to your twelve-week Vital Vision is, therefore, the focus of this *Sip*. We begin by exploring some of the emotional and psychological preparation that is required for success and examine what happens if this foundation is not in place.

Expanding Beyond Your Comfort Zone
Forewarned is Forearmed

Stepping into the success of your Vital Vision requires you to step out of your comfort zone. This can feel highly emotional and many people are unprepared for the range of de-stabilizing emotions that can arise in the early stages of attaining success. Additionally, people often find ways of potentially destroying their success and therefore happiness, either just before the successful Vital Vision is about to materialize or immediately after it's consolidated. During a recent house move, I discovered that I'm not immune.

Comfort Zone

A feeling of psychological, emotional and physical safety.

The Lake House
Sabotaging Success

I had the good fortune to live in a lake house for many years. However, the time came when Tim and I were tired of the constant upkeep of the shoreline and garden, so we decided to move to a nearby townhouse. However, immediately after moving, I fell into a funk. The new house didn't feel quite right and my mind and heart kept wandering back to the lake house. I even found myself taking drives to check on the old place, especially a beloved cherry tree that grew in the front garden that I had tended since planting it as a tender sapling.

You can imagine my horror when I discovered that the new owners had chopped down the much-loved tree. My funk now descended into a deeper malaise that I couldn't shift even when Tim suggested that we take a month-long vacation in Arizona. My immediate response was horror. Stuck in my difficult feelings, I shared my thoughts with Marilyn, a trusted friend. I asked her, 'why would I want to spend a month in Arizona? What would I do with all that time?' After several conversations, she asked me, 'why did you and Tim decide to sell the lake house?' I was able to answer instantly, 'to free ourselves up from the constant upkeep of the place.' A few moments of silence followed as I reflected on these words before the moment of insight. My breakthrough rose to awareness. I smiled with a mixture of sheepishness and happiness. 'Oh!' I laughed with embarrassment, 'I wanted more time and made a big sacrifice to achieve it yet when I got it, I didn't feel comfortable or positive with it. In fact, I felt resentful.'

This was true, I'd experienced the successful transition into my dream vision as painful and depressing yet, actually, it was deeper than that. Reflecting on how I'd lived a very busy life that included running a home, being a parent and wife as well as holding down a demanding corporate job, I realized that attaining my goal of extra time came as a shock. It brought me into connection with a luxury that I'd never fully experienced, i.e. time. Unconsciously, this felt scary. What do we do when we're scared? We fight, flee or freeze. In my case, I'd frozen in the safety of staying attached to the familiar, and therefore safe, past by:

- Looking back at my old home with longing.
- Remaining attached to the cherry tree.
- Maintaining a defensive refusal to step into the joy of my successful creation of more time as marked by the vacation.

It's interesting to note that even though I was able to live a clearly secure life, I was not immune to sabotaging success and happiness.

Does this resonate with you?

On reflection, I was able to understand that moving away from the security of my old home had stretched me beyond of my emotional comfort zone. In order to enjoy my success, I had to make the necessary psychological adjustments. Once I'd done that, I was able to let go of my attachment to my old house and enjoy living in my new home. Shifting into the success of your Vital Vision will require similar adjustments. Let's explore your experiences with success.

Coffee Time!

Tell me one memory of success. It can be recent or something that happened as far back as early childhood.

....

....

The Feeling of Success

In workshops, I often find that participants use feelings when describing their experience of success. For example:

- I feel happy.
- I feel independent.
- I feel fun.
- I feel adventurous to be finally going solo backpacking.
- I feel peaceful living in harmony with nature.
- I feel compassion.
- I feel safe having sufficient money.
- I feel humbled to understand, and to be honoring, my life purpose.
- I feel relieved to be free from childhood traumas.
- I feel nourished now that I am taking time for my favorite hobby.

Recalling a Memory of Success

Tell me, using your above memory, how did success make you feel?

....

....

....

....

....

....

....

....

....

....

....

....

....

Tell me, what top three emotions would you like to always feel in moments of success?

1.

2.

3.

Sabotaging Success

> ### The Shift Café Definition of Sabotage
>
> The act of spoiling a longed-for accomplishment.

Tell me, can you describe a time when you have sabotaged your long-for success?

Reflect on thoughts, actions or feelings that you experienced at the time.

....

....

....

Tell me, what was the reason for this sabotaging behavior?

Often, until we become aware of our self-sabotaging habits, we repeat them. Taking time now to become clear on your habits may prove invaluable in helping you honor your Shift Step Actions and successful attainment of your Vital Vision.

....

....

....

Tell me, can you think of three ways to guard against self-sabotaging your future Vital Vision Success?

1.

2.

3.

The Shift Café Vital Vision Success Guide

Knowing where you currently stand in relation to your Vital Vision Success will help you work out your next Shift Action Steps towards success.

Tell me, what level of success do you currently feel in relation to your Vital Vision?

....

....

....

Use **The Shift Café Vital Vision Success Guide** below to help you and circle the level that you feel applies.

The Shift Café Vital Vision Success Guide

5: Joyful: I feel delighted with my current level of success.

4: Confident: I know that I'm very close to attaining success in attaining my Vital Vision.

3: Self Trust: I sense that I will become successful with my Vital Vision. I fully trust that the wisdom and clarity required for my Shift Action Steps, leading to success, are arriving.

2: Hopeful: Although I'm unclear of my next Shift Action Steps that will lead to the successful attainment of my Vital Vision, I feel hopeful that the clarity/breakthrough will arrive.

1: Stuck: I feel the yearning for the successful attainment of my Vital Vision yet I'm unsure of my next Shift Action Step. Or: I know what Shift Action Steps I need to take to ensure the success of my Vital Vision yet find myself unwilling, or unable, to follow through.

0: Hopeless: I fear I'll never be able to successfully attain my Vital Vision.

Personal Definition of Vital Vision Success

You now have a clear insight into:

- How success feels to you.
- How and why you sabotage success.
- How successful you currently feel in relation to attaining your Vital Vision.

Write a short statement that defines your personal definition of Vital Vision success.

Vital Vision success for me means ....

....

I will know I am successful because ....

....

I will feel:

-
-
-

I will guard against sabotage by:

-
-
-

Place this statement in your Serenity Basket. It will help you on your Shift Café journey.

I place a fresh log on the fire, eyeing a vase of winter flowers I placed on my coffee table a few days ago. Checking the water level, I notice they are still fresh. With constant watering, they continue to blossom. It occurred to me how success can be like these flowers. If they had no water they would wither, yet with constant attention they thrive. Returning to my desk, I notice how the noonday sun has reached its full height for this time of year, just brushing the canopy of the hickory trees. Soft white clouds float across the sky.

The Shift Café Sketching Corner

Winter Sky and Noonday Sun

Draw a picture of the winter sky with soft clouds and gentle sunlight. **Label** them with notes on how Vital Vision success looks and feels to you. **Journal** on what will require your constant care and attention.

Place this picture in your Serenity Basket.
It will help you to remember throughout The Shift Café journey that the sun can shine on your dreams!

My foot accidentally knocks the Serenity Basket causing a long white swan feather to fall. I'm not quite sure how it arrived in the basket. I gather it in my hands where it brushes against my fingers. This gentleness is a timely and fitting reminder. There may be times on The Shift Café journey where you come up against difficult or painful memories or realizations. In these moments, it's crucial to treat yourself with immense kindness.

Nurturing Success – Vital Vision Shift Action Step

Success
The attainment
of your Vital
Vision to a
level that feels
rewarding.

Tell me, what *Success* focused Vital Vision Shift Action Step will you take this week?

....

....
Stretch
beyond your
comfort zone.

....

Tell me, at what level are you going to honor this Shift Action Step in the coming week?

Make the
necessary
psychological
adjustments.

1   2   3   4   5   6   7   8   9   10

Tell me, how will this support the successful attainment of your Vital Vision?

....
Success

....
requires constant
loving

....
care and
attention.

Serenity Basket Heart Wisdom

Reflect on this question:

From what I've learned today, does my heart have any further wisdom that will help me to attain my Vital Vision?

....

....

....

Place this guidance into your Serenity Basket. Let it help you on your journey through *The Shift Café*.

Congratulations! In this *Sip*, you have:

- Created your personal definition of success in relation to your Vital Vision.
- Explored how success can be consciously or unconsciously sabotaged.

Remember:

Defining success in relation to your Vital Vision gives you a clear picture of what you wish to achieve and will help you know when it's been attained.

In the next *Shift Café Sip*, you'll identify the team of people who will help you attain your Vital Vision success. I ask you: **Tell Me**, Who's in Your Shift Café Crew? See you there!

LEAF

by Andrew Roberts

Leaf is falling from
the tree,
descending
travelling in time,
perfection in motion
as the autumnal breeze
sings so gently
with the weeping
flower.

Leaf looks upwards
smiling at the fading
sun which hides
behind grey skies
and the birds will fly
homeward,
In evening time Leaf
shall dream under
the stars,
Leaf shall return
to the tree

come Springtime,
her journey will
begin once more
in silence
and in
synchronicity.

Eternal poetry
shall be written
so very beautifully
by the hand of
nature
and on this night
which we await
the Moon
shall rise
again.

Between The Sips

An opportunity to pause between the main *Sips* so
that you can focus on common limiting beliefs and
actions that prevent Vital Visions being attained.

Throughout *The Shift Café* journey, you're gathering many insights and strategies to help you create your Vital Vision. This may sometimes feel like the type of quest found in all good hero/ine stories where, typically, the main character is challenged by a series of hurdles that need to be overcome. In my work, these obstacles generally show up as explanations for why a Vital Vision can't be attained. I've identified the four M.O.S.T common reasons cited for not stepping into the Level 10 version of a Vital Vision:

M = Money
O = Overwhelm
S = Self-Care
T = Time

If you resonate with any of the above, these Between the Sips pauses throughout the journey will be especially helpful. Drawing on knowledge and guidance from guest writers, who are experts in their fields, you'll reflect on your relationship with each reason so that you can eliminate the fear, procrastination and self-sabotage that comes with them. Instead, you will develop the confidence, courage and resilience to push beyond your current self-imposed limits.

You may be like Sarah who began *The Shift Café* journey overwhelmed by despair, fearing she would never find the job that matches her expertise. Or, perhaps, you'll be like Colette who has a secret vision of becoming more politically active yet believes that being a busy mother diminishes the time available for such pursuits. However, using the Between the Sips activities, both women identified their limiting beliefs and overcame crucial sabotaging hurdles that had been blocking their Vital Vision success. I fully trust that this will be the same for you. You'll shortly be exploring the first most common obstacle cited for not stepping fully into Vital Visions. Before that, take a moment to examine your M.O.S.T common limiting beliefs that hinder you from attaining your Vital Vision.

Tell me, which of the M.O.S.T common reasons hold you back from stepping into your Level 10 Vital Vision? **Circle** those that apply. Don't worry if you circle all of them!

Money   *Overwhelm*   *Self-care*   *Time*

If none of these apply, what do you feel is your M.O.S.T common reason for not stepping into your Vital Vision?

....

....

....

Now that you've briefly identified what obstacles or limiting beliefs are holding you back, you can look forward to the Between The Sips pauses throughout the book that will help you examine more deeply your reasons for them and how they can be overcome. We begin with reason #1 = Money.

#1 M = Money

Many people are especially good at believing that they aren't allowed to invest money in their own well-being and visions. I regularly hear:

- My spouse/partner/children/grandchildren won't like it if I spend the money.
- I need to save for emergencies/a rainy day/the future.
- It's the children's inheritance; I can't spend it on myself.

Of course, it's important to have financial savvy, savings and safety. However, many people don't invest in themselves financially as they lack confidence and experience with money. Additionally, our patriarchal society is geared to keep not only women, but also men, in a place of financial lack, fear and inferiority.

Infusing Money with the Energy of Love

In *The Shift Café*, we believe it's helpful to change your mindset about money so that you thoughtfully use finances to support your Vital Vision. To help with this, I'd like to share an article written by Astra, a wealth expert, about the healing properties of money.

The Healing Properties of Money
By wealth expert, Astra

I often come across people who hold an underlying belief that money is bad or unhelpful. I used to hold this belief until I became aware of it, pried it loose from eons of being buried, and released it. It took work – it was a challenge – but it is gone, gone, gone! I now choose to infuse money with the energy of love. For the purpose of this article, I will focus on the physical and energetic healing reasons why I love money. Simply put, money is a gift from nature. The saying goes: 'money doesn't grow on trees.' This is true – however, paper money DOES grow from plants! Equally as cool, metal money is harvested from Mother Earth herself.

First, I will focus on U.S. paper bills. Recently it dawned on me that I didn't know exactly how the bills were made, so I did a little Google research. It turns out that flax plant fibers make up 25% of each U.S. paper dollar. Plants are healing. Most of us are familiar with sprinkling flaxseed on our salads and adding flax oil to recipes to reap the health benefits of the omega-3 fatty acids. The remaining 75% of the bill comes from cotton. What I didn't know was that, in addition to spinning beautiful fabric, the cotton plant also has its place in the world of physical healing! The cotton root is used for urinary problems, while an infusion made from the leaves of the cotton plant can be used to combat inflammation. The extract from the leaves is used for healing wounds, and the crushed leaves and flowers can be used to soothe pain from burns. An infusion made from cotton seeds can be used to help reduce pain during menstruation. I'm blown away by the cotton plant! Studying all this feels so healing when I think about physical money! But wait, there's more. Now we cover U.S. coinage. Coins are currently made of:

- **Pennies:** 97.5% zinc plated with a thin layer of copper.

- **Nickels:** a solid alloy of 75% copper and 25% nickel.

- **Dimes, quarters, half-dollars:** 2 outer layers of 75% copper and 25% nickel bonded to a core of solid copper, for an overall content of about 92% copper.

- **Dollars:** manganese brass bonded to a copper core; overall content 88.5% copper, 6% zinc, 3.5% Manganese, 2% nickel.

Wow! So the main metals used to make coins are: zinc, copper, nickel, and manganese.

Here are some of the healing properties of each metal:

Zinc: Helps improve immune function, speeds the healing of wounds and eases diarrhea.

Copper: When worn on the body, copper is thought to improve such inflammatory conditions as arthritis and rheumatism. It's also thought to cleanse the organs and immune system.

Nickel: The healing properties of nickel are thought to include cleansing, stimulation of the liver, soothing headaches and easing fear, as well as promoting the energy of playfulness!

Manganese: Helpful for the brain, nerves and muscles, and supportive of the reproductive system and mammary glands.

Money, the 'root of all evil'?

I wouldn't bet on it — not for all the money in the world!

All the money in the world?

I'm feeling healthier already!

Coffee Time!

Tell me, which aspect of your Vital Vision requires some nourishment in relation to money?

....

....

....

Tell me, which of your gifts do you wish to gift to others so that they can achieve?

....

....

....

Tell me, how does Astra's article change your feelings towards investing money in your Vital Vision? If so, how?

....

....

....

Nurturing Dreams- Vital Vision Shift Action Step

Budgeting is a valuable part of your financial health. feelings that do.

Allow your finances to support your Vital Vision.

Tell me, what *Money* focused Shift Action Step will you take this week?

....

....

....

Money is a gift from nature.

Tell me, how is this going to support the successful implementation of your Vital Vision?

....

....

....

Metal money is harvested from Mother Earth

Tell me, at what level are you going to honor this Nurturing Money Action Step in the week?

Money is the root of all evil

    1   **2**   **3**   **4**   **5**   **6**   **7**   **8**   **9**   **10**

Remember:

Money, the root of all evil'?
I wouldn't bet on it — not for all the money in the world!

We now return to your next *Sip*, where we will gather around *The Shift Café* table where I ask you: **Tell Me**, Who's in Your Shift Café Crew? See You There!

Contemplation Nook

Sip 6
Nurturing Connection

Not for ourselves are we born.
Cicero

The Shift Café Definition of Connection

The ability to open your heart and attend to the
needs of another from a place of love –
and to be able to receive this love..

Mid-morning In The Shift Café
Swan

The swan feather rests between my fingers. Its gentleness touches my heart. Instead of rushing ahead with my work as I may normally do, I'm drawn to pause and slow down. I notice how the feather is both fragile and strong. I contemplate its many functions including keeping the swan warm and dry, to help it take flight and to support its fight for protection against any perceived threat. I recall the two swans on the lake. Loyal and monogamous, they'll be mates for life. At breeding time next spring, the male, unlike many other creatures in nature, will take an active role in building the nest on which the female will lay her eggs. How loyally he will stay by her side at this time, bringing her food and fending off potential predators. He even takes his turn at incubating the eggs.

 Once hatched, he will, like the mother swan, take his turn at allowing the chicks to ride on his back as they search for food. With this male swan by her side, the female knows that in the fragile world of nature, she has a faithful partner by her side ready to support her in her most vulnerable times. Should the need arise, he will fight for her and their chicks. They work as a loyal team with a constant focus on high quality existence, protection, support and survival — all of which allows them to flourish. How many of us humans feel the same level of protection and support in our lives? More importantly, how many of us take the time to consciously reflect on the quality of people with who we surround ourselves? Do you ever ask yourself:

Who do I allow into my circle?
How do they serve me?
Do they really have my best interests at heart?

I take up my pen and write the question for today's Sip:

Tell Me, Who's in Your Shift Café Crew?

Tell Me, Who's in your Shift Café Crew?

Intention

~⅌~∽~⅌~⅌~∽~⅌~∽~

To identify the ideal members of your Shift
Café Super Deluxe Delight Crew.

In the last *Sip*, you:

Success

- Created your personal definition of success in relation to your Vital Vision.
- Explored how success can be consciously or unconsciously sabotaged.

The attainment of your Vital Vision to a level that feels rewarding. solutions to a situation that feels stuck.

Tell me, at what level did you honor *Success* focused Shift Action Step this week?

1   2   3   4   5   6   7   8   9   10

What worked for you?   Why?
What didn't work for you?   Why not?
What do you still need to do?

....

....

....

....

....

....

....

Tell me, how did this help to support the overall development of your Vital Vision?

....

....

....

....

....

....

....

....

Finding Your Ideal *Shift Café Super Deluxe Delight Crew*

The Cheerleaders for Your Success

Identifying what your Vital Vision success will look and feel like is an important component of *The Shift Café* journey. Additionally, you also need a group of supportive people acting as cheerleaders for your success. I want you to be surrounded by trustworthy people so that whenever you get stuck you can turn to a range of top-quality people for honest advice. They'll help you step into your Vital Vision at the highest level, ensuring that you truly stretch into the POWER of your POTENTIAL. I call this team your *Shift Café Super Deluxe Delight Crew.*

The Shift Café Definition of
Super Deluxe Delight Crew

Your chosen community of high quality, trustworthy and supportive people, pets, activities and locations.

Sometimes, you'll require the expertise of a professional, such as a banker or lawyer. Other times you may need a close friend in who you can confide. These crew members will help you when your fears, doubts or confusions are saying:

I can't ...
I'm stuck ...
I don't know how ...
I failed again ...

Today, you'll explore the core attributes required within your *Shift Café Deluxe Delight Crew* and identify the people who can fulfill these roles. These may be people who are already valuable members of your current support crew. You may also identify new types of people you need to seek. Additionally, you may discover that some people in your current crew are not truly serving your highest well-being. You will, perhaps, need to make decisions about the level of involvement they have on your journey to Vital Vision success. For example, Tiffany, a recent Shift Café participant, described how the activities in this *Sip* helped her weed out toxic people, stating, 'I now only allow positive people in my life.'

Can Only People be in my Shift Café Crew?

No! As you know by now, my dog Bailey is a huge support to me. He's a constant companion providing comfort, especially in difficult times. He comes high on the list of members in my Shift Café Super Deluxe Delight Crew alongside my husband, son and daughter-in-law. Many people include pets in their Shift Café crew. Other people include activities and locations. For example, your crew might include a favorite place or activities such as a forest or walking in nature. Your supportive settings and activities can be as crucial as people. Don't forget about your inspirational person from *Sip 2,* they can also be part of your crew. Any person, living or dead, real or fictional, who you find inspirational in moments of difficulty can be part of your support team. One recent participant, Sarah, included characters from her favorite video games!

Can I Only Have One Crew?

You can have just one crew to support your whole adult life, or separate crews for different areas and times of your life. For example, the support crew a mother with a toddler might choose is, perhaps, very different from the crew she'll select when she's a grandmother. I've had several Super Deluxe Delight crews over the years, including when setting up my business. Initially, I would run things by my friend, Marilyn. With her Bachelor's degree in Mathematics, Master's degree in Management and experience as a Plant Manager, she approached issues from the perspective of processes and strategies. However, she would also ask: 'what tools are needed for the success of the participants?' Additionally, I would run written components by Kathy who had a degree majoring in English. Two other crew members, Judy and Holly, used their expertise in sales and social media to support my marketing strategy. Another member of my crew is Paul. Preferring a quiet and simple pace of life, he spends his free time tending vegetables. Much of the best guidance I've received in my most stuck or saddest times has come while drinking a cup of coffee with Paul, sitting on a rickety bench overlooking his latest crop. Each of these people became invaluable members of my first business crew. They remain so today.

Swans understand the importance of crews. They don't only gather on water but will also flock together in fields where the pasture is full of nourishment. By coming together in this way, they're affording themselves the protection found in numbers from natural predators. They understand the primal survival component of being connected to others who understand their needs and requirements for a safe and healthy life. They actively seek out their crew — not any crew but a crew that would, if necessary, fight for their survival.

Tell me, can you think of any other animals who support each other as the swans do? What can you learn from them? Journal your thoughts in the box below.

Coffee Time!

How To Identify Your *Deluxe Delight Shift Café Crew*

Look at these two cups of coffee.

The cup on the left is a basic cup of coffee, an everyday brew. The one on the right is *The Shift Café Super Deluxe Delight*. From the sweet sugar granules at its base to the marshmallows and sprinkles on the whipped cream, it's the full deal! Each of these cups of coffee represents a potential type of crew. The original brew represents a crew that feels satisfactory yet you know there are ways it could be improved. *The Shift Café Super Deluxe Delight* coffee represents a super power crew, full of the highest quality members that offer inspirational support. On the table overleaf, see how each component of the *Shift Café Deluxe Delight Coffee* represents a specific type of personality trait required by top quality *Shift Café Deluxe Delight Crew* members. Read the descriptions carefully. In the empty right hand columns, answer the questions.

Aspect of the Coffee Crew	Role in the Crew	Who, if anyone, currently serves this role?	Are they doing a good job? Yes/No?	Who would you like to fulfill this role? Feel free to add a new person if the current person in this role no longer feels appropriate
Saucer	**The Expansive Supporter** This grounded person sturdily, quietly and consistently supports and encourages you.			
Spoon	**The Stirrer** This person can positively stir things up, having the ability to see a range of perspectives. This person will also allow you to gripe, moan and complain but only for a limited period before shifting towards forward thinking positive solutions.			
Cup/Glass	**The Safe Container** This person will listen and empathize with your fears and anxieties yet will encourage you to find ways to move forward with courage.			
Sugar Granules	**The Sweet Cheerleader** This is the person who brings some sweetness to the Vital Vision journey. They lift you up with laughter in spite of adversity.			

The Boiling Water	**The Active Visionary** This is the adventurous person who sees your long-term visions clearly and identifies how they can be brought to life in logical and easy to manage steps.			
The Milk	**The Soother** This person is able to calm you down when you are anxious or have been overdoing it.			
The Cream	**The Connector** This person will have a wide range of contacts and be able to suggest with whom you can speak to solve a dilemma.			
The Sprinkles	**The Professionals** In many cafés, the sprinkles on a coffee are served as optional extras. At The Shift Café, we consider the sprinkles to be a vital component of any responsible Deluxe Delight Coffee and Shift Café Crew. These are the professional people who provide support in the following areas: • Finances • Law • Administration • Mental and physical health.			

The Biscotti	The Explorer			
	This person is someone who will let you explore confused thoughts in a safe space. They won't judge, criticize or reject you while you work things through. They respect confidentiality.			
The Marshmallows	The Compassionate Guide This is the person you turn to when mistakes have happened or the project feels like it's fallen apart. They remain calm, asking: • What have you learned from this experience? • Moving forward, what is your very next step?			
The Creamer Jug	The Time Gifter This person understands the importance of allowing time and space for ideas to be discussed. They willingly give you the time to allow ideas to expand and evolve			

The Extra Cream	The Kind Heart			
	This is the person you can call at 3:00am knowing they will definitely answer and want to listen. When times are tough, they will call you up, send you messages, create random acts of kindness that remind you that you are loved, liked, and valued.			
Tell Me, is there anything else you would add to your Shift Café Deluxe Delight Coffee?	What Roles Would They Play in Your Crew?			*Who is the person that would take this role in your crew?*

The Shift Café Sketching Corner

Your *Super Deluxe Delight Crew*

In the image below, **color the two cups of coffee.**
Label according to your answers from the previous activity.
Journal any insights gained. For example,

- Are you surprised by who is part of your *Shift Café Super Deluxe Delight Crew*?
- Have you discovered that some of your current crew members do not meet the required quality to be part of your *Shift Café Super Deluxe Delight Crew*? How will you handle this?
- Which types of crew members are missing from your *Shift Café Super Deluxe Delight Crew*?
- Is one person taking on all the roles?

Many married women I work with often tell me that their husband fulfills many, if not all, of the roles required within the *Shift Café Super Deluxe Delight Crew*. If this applies to you, I invite you to stretch beyond this. Who else could fill these roles?

Tell me, based on your notes, what three words summarize who or what you want in your *Shift Café Super Deluxe Delight* coffee crew?

1.

2.

3.

Tell me, how can you use these words to guide future decisions when selecting members of your *Shift Café Super Deluxe Delight* crew?

....

....

....

....

....

....

....

....

....

....

....

Place your picture in your Serenity Basket.
It will help you to remember throughout The Shift Café journey that the sky really is your limit!

Nurturing Connection – Vital Vision Shift Action Step

Connection

The ability to open your heart and attend to the needs of another from a place of love – and to be able to receive this love.

Tell me, what *Connection* focused Vital Vision Shift Action Step will you take this week?

Take the time to consciously reflect on the quality of people with who you surround yourself.

....

....

....

Tell me, at what level are you going to honor this Shift Action Step in the coming week?

Who consistently supports and encourages you?

1   2   3   4   5   6   7   8   9   10

Tell me, how will this support the successful attainment of your Vital Vision?

You can have just one crew to support your whole adult life, or separate crews for different areas and stages of your life.

....

....

....

Serenity Basket Heart Wisdom
Reflect on this question:

From what I've learned today, does my heart have any further wisdom
that will help me to attain my Vital Vision?

....

....

....

Place this guidance into your Serenity Basket. Let it help you on your journey
through *The Shift Café*.

Congratulations! In this *Sip*, you have:

- Explored how to nurture good quality connections.
- Identified the ideal members of your Shift Café Super Deluxe Delight
  crew.

Remember:

> *Your Shift Café Super Deluxe Delight Crew will help you stretch
> into the POWER of your POTENTIAL.*

*I return the swan feather to the Serenity Basket, thanking it for today's inspiration.
It's time to decorate my home in preparation for those who will be shortly gathering
for Thanksgiving.*

In the next *Sip*, we shift the focus as I ask you: **Tell Me**, How Do You Support
Others? See you there!

Seedling

by Christy Dance-Greenhut

A tiny seed deep in the ground,
sees nothing but darkness when it looks around.
Yet, rather than thinking, *I'm stuck in a rut and all alone,*
it yearns for something that it's never known.

It has faith that beyond the rut there is more to see,
and that growth can bring a new reality.
It believes with all its might that it has somewhere to go.
Then, a miracle happens. It begins to grow.
Its shell that has grown hard begins to crack,
despite, or perhaps because of, the pressure on its back.

It will grow roots and continue to thrive,
long before someone notices that it's still alive.
It takes what it needs and nothing more,
leaving nutrients behind so that others may soar.

The warmth of the sun guides its direction,
as it leaves the hard shell that has provided protection.
Little by little, the seed continues to grow,
creating more seeds for the wind to blow.

Contemplation Nook

Sip 7
Nurturing Reflection

If you can, show them the better way.
If you cannot, remember that this is why you have the gift of kindness.

Marcus Aurelius

The Shift Café Definition of Reflection

The ability to look at your own actions, thoughts and beliefs
with honesty & integrity so that you can show up in life for
yourself, and others, at the highest and most enjoyable level.

Midday In The Shift Café
Squirrel

My home has been cleaned in the preceding days and food gathered. Later today my family and friends are gathering to celebrate Thanksgiving. This is our annual festival of gratitude where we give thanks for the harvest and other blessings we've received throughout the preceding year. From the Serenity Basket, I retrieve the pine cones and spruce branches gathered on my dawn walk and position them as decorations by the fire and as arched boughs of welcome over the front door.

Placing individual pine cones by each placemat at the dining table, I think of who will be gathered including my husband, Tim, along with my son, Brandon, and his wife, Heather. Some of my most trusted friends are also coming and, of course, Bailey! Naturally, there are others who can't be here who are also in my heart including Aunt Florence and my mother as well as my dear niece who lives faraway in Chicago. Each of these are, in their unique ways, deeply valued members of my Shift Café Super Deluxe Delight Crew.

Having put the final touches to the dining table, I take a moment to rest and reflect in my Shift Café Contemplation Nook. Full of gratitude, I sip my coffee made with freshly roasted beans and topped with a swirl of extra cream and sprinkles while watching a squirrel dart across the lawn. Leaping onto a heavy branch, she kicks up fountains of powdery snow with her tiny yet sharp hind claws as she scales the trunk before disappearing among the branches. No doubt she has retrieved some nourishing nuts and is now returning to a safe place of warmth for a long sleep. Squirrels instinctively know that in winter they must conserve their energy, concentrating solely on essential activities that support a good quality existence — and survival. As humans, many of us have lost this self-care instinct. This is especially so for those of us who are often over generous with our time, skills and energy. Does this resonate with you?

In today's Sip, our focus is on how you contribute to a Shift Café Deluxe Delight crew for those you love. However, while it's important that you contribute to the crews of others, it's also important to ensure that these crews respect your values, skills, time and energy. This is even more important as we age. We simply don't have the time, energy and, perhaps, desire to squander on people or activities that do not value or respect us. Therefore, to ensure that you are gifting your uniquely precious gifts and times wisely, in this Sip I ask you:

Tell Me, How Do You Contribute as a Crew Member?

How Do You Contribute as a Crew Member?

INTENTION

To identify:

1. Where, how and why you're showing up as a crew member at a basic level.
2. Where, how and why you're showing up as a crew member at a Super Deluxe Delight level.

In the last *Sip*, you:

- Explored how to nurture good quality connections.
- Identified the ideal members of your Shift Café Super Deluxe Delight crew.

Tell me, at what level did you honor your *Connection* focused Shift Action Step this week?

1   2   3   4   5   6   7   8   9   10

What worked for you?   Why?

What didn't work for you?   Why not?

What do you still need to do?

Super Deluxe Delight Crew

Your chosen community of high quality, trustworthy and supportive people, activities, locations, and pets.

....

....

....

Tell me, how did this help to support the overall development of your Vital Vision?

....

....

....

How To Become a High Quality Shift Café Deluxe Delight Crew Member

In *Sip 6*, you focused on the people you would like to select for prominent roles in your *Shift Café Deluxe Delight Crew*. You learned how creating a *Shift Café Super Deluxe Delight Crew* would help you stretch into the POWER of your POTENTIAL. In this *Sip*, you'll reflect on how, as a high quality supportive member of a Deluxe Delight Crew, you have the POWER to support others as they step into their POTENTIAL. Here in *The Shift Café* we firmly believe that giving is as important as receiving. While ensuring that your time, skills and energy are being respected, being a crew member is a vital part of the legacy you're giving others during your lifetime.

Take another look at these images of two types of coffee.

Remember:

The cup on the left is a basic cup of coffee, an everyday brew. The one on the right is *The Shift Café Super Deluxe Delight* and represents a super power crew, full of the highest quality members that offer inspirational support. Unlike the squirrel that remains in tune with how to conserve her energy, we often give away too much time and energy to others, depleting ourselves in the process. Maintaining a fair balance between those who truly need us and our own self-care can be tough.

Respect

As you reflect on your role as a crew member, be sure to think about who truly respects you, who may be taking advantage of you and how skilled you are at protecting yourself while also giving your best. Use the coffee images above to help you reflect on your level and quality of contribution to the crews of which you are currently a member. Let's explore.

Coffee Time!

Tell me, in which crews do you currently contribute?
Family? Friends? Community? Neighbors?
Clubs/Societies? College/Work?

-

-

-

Tell me, in which of these crews are you currently contributing at the basic everyday brew level?

....

....

....

Tell me, why are you currently contributing at this basic level?

....

....

....

Tell me, what do you need to do about this? Step up or step back?

....

....

....

Where are you Super Deluxe Delight Rocking It?

Tell me, in which crews do you currently contribute at a *Shift Café Deluxe Delight* level?

Get specific. Which component most suits you? Are you a sprinkle or a spoon? For example, Shama, a member of my pilot study group for this book, identified herself as a cup, spoon and the cream. Look back at the definitions in the table in *Sip 6* to help you.

I excel at the following *Deluxe Delight* Crew member skills:

-
-
-
-

The Shift Café Sketching Corner

How Do You Excel as a Super Deluxe Delight Crew Member?

Color *the Shift Café Deluxe Delight* coffee again, only this time label and make notes reflecting on your own skills and contributions to any crews in which you currently belong. Make notes on areas for improvement and on those of which you are most proud.

....

....

....

Place this in your Serenity Basket. Let it guide you throughout The Shift Café journey, ensuring that you are thoughtfully utilizing your time, energy and skills as a crew member in ways that are enjoyable and beneficial to you and the person/people you are supporting.

Gratitude

There's no doubt that having people in our *Super Deluxe Delight Crew*, and being part of a crew, is a blessing. We gain life-enhancing nourishment and support in the deep connections forged by such close friendships. Find some time today to treat yourself to a *Super Deluxe Delight* coffee. Use your very best beans or granules. Once made, take yourself to a quiet space in your garden or local park. If you prefer, visit a café that serves your favorite coffee. Try to find one with an outdoor garden space that overlooks trees. As you connect with Mother Nature, savoring the flavor of your drink, take notice of the coffee's different elements such as the spoon, cup or glass. As you drink, think of the connection and reflection focused activities you've completed in this and *Sip 6*. Reflect on the people you've identified who take on these important roles in your *Shift Café Deluxe Delight Crew* and for whom you play these roles.

Tell me, how can you show your gratitude to these valuable people in your life?

....

....

....

....

....

....

....

....

The doorbell rings. Bailey barks excitedly, attempting to beat me to the door to welcome our guests. As we welcome each other with hugs and kisses, the sweet aroma of the pine tree bough arching over the door dances around us. Ushering my guests into the warmth for a welcome drink, I recall the early morning view from the ledge on Gratitude Hill. Soon we will sit around the table and feast on our meal for Thanksgiving. My joyful heart feels deeply blessed. As we toast the blessings of the year, I'll also silently raise my glass to the squirrel sleeping in the tree, thanking her for the inspiration for today's Sip.

Nurturing Reflection– Vital Vision Shift Action Step

Reflection

The ability to look at your own actions, thoughts and beliefs with honesty & integrity.

Tell me, what *Reflection* focused Vital Vision Shift Action Step will you take this week?

....

Honor

....

your

values.

....

Tell me, at what level are you going to honor your *Reflection* focused Shift Action Step this week?

Respect
Your
1   2   3   4   5   6   7   8   9   10   *Time*

Tell me, how will this support the successful attainment of your Vital Vision?

....

....

How are
you valuing
others?

....

Serenity Basket Heart Wisdom

Reflect on this question:

From what I've learned today, does my heart have any further wisdom that will help me to attain my Vital Vision?

....

....

Congratulations! In this *Sip*, you've identified:

- Where, how and why you're showing up as a crew member at a basic level?
- Where, how and why you're showing up as a crew member at a Super Deluxe Delight level?

Remember:

Your Shift Café Super Deluxe Delight Crew will help you stretch into the POWER of your POTENTIAL — and you have the POWER to do the same for others.

In the Contemplation Nook today, you've focused on how you support others. Knowing where you need support and how you support others is a crucial component of your Vital Vision success. These crew members help us when we're feeling stuck and celebrate with us when we succeed. Sometimes, however, even with great people around us we become super stuck in negative thought patterns, beliefs and actions. This is known as a fixed-mindset.

In the next *Sip*, you're journeying deep into *The Shift Café* forest where we'll meet fireflies as I ask you: **Tell Me**, *How Can You Shift from a Fixed Mindset to a Growth Mindset.* See You There!

Nature

by Zarley Lawson

Not a worry in sight
Only peace seeping through the light

The light brightens a display of colorful flowers
Adding a subtle touch to nature's powers

The flowers are surrounded by enormous trees
Masking a beautiful gentle breeze

The breeze causes the leaves to sway
Like someone showing the way

Over the trees, hills hide behind another hill
Like they are stuck in time, shy and still

Forming a beautiful scene, crafted without a flaw
A true bite of nature, safe space to withdraw

Sounds scatter in every direction
Bouncing back, like a mirror's reflection

The birds chatter in beat, like a melody to a song
Followed by a woodpecker trying to find a place to belong

A harmony that's breathtaking
Like a masterpiece in the making

An experience that one can reminisce as a treat
However, like reality, someone can't hit repeat.

Contemplation Nook

Sip 8
Nurturing Growth Mindset

If you do not change direction, you may end up where you're heading.

Chinese Proverb

The Shift Café Definition of Mindset

The beliefs and thoughts that affect how you
choose to feel and react to any situation.

Thanksgiving Evening
The Forest, a Broken Heart and some Fireflies.

Our Thanksgiving meal was a huge success. After dinner, we sat around the fire as I asked my favorite Thanksgiving question. It's one you know: Tell me, what is the one thing for which you are most grateful? Brandon groaned.

'Oh Mom, we do this every year. And every year we say the same things. Can't you think of anything more original?'

'Okay,' I said. 'Let's go for a walk instead.'

Soon they were following me out of the garden, through the gates and along the path winding around the Vital Vision Lake until we came to the forest where earlier I collected the pine branches.

'I haven't been here for years,' said Brandon.

'Follow me.' I took off, taking a different track to the usual path, attempting to push

back brambles as I went. Both Tim and Brandon attempted to dissuade me.

'It's too brambly, you'll never get through.'

Only Heather seemed to understand. She joined me up front holding her flashlight aloft so that I was able to see the tangled thicket clearly, my glove protecting me from the thorns. At a particularly stubborn spot Brandon withdrew the pocket knife he often carried with him, a habit from his time as an Eagle Scout. Before long, despite the darkening sky, we made a breakthrough cutting through into a small clearing.

'What's this?' Tim, Brandon and Heather were stupefied.

Standing before us was a small log cabin, covered in brambles.

'What is this place?'
'How long has it been here?'
'How come I never knew about this place?'

The questions came thick and fast. Brandon was incredulous. He simply couldn't believe that during the whole of his childhood playing on this land that he'd never come across the cabin before. Heather shone her flashlight at different sections where a fusion of shadow and light outlined a tiny door and two windows that, surprisingly, given how long they'd been there, were still intact. Perhaps the brambles and surrounding spruce trees had protected them.

'Remember,' I asked, 'how I always told you not to enter this part of the forest?'

'I do. Why couldn't I? I would've loved to have played here.'

'I know. I now regret that I didn't let you.'

'Mom, you've got to tell me. Whose cabin was this? How come I've never known about it?'

'This cabin belonged to my father,' I replied. 'The reason I never told you about it was because I didn't want you to spend time in a place where a man like my father spent time.' It was true. I explained:

'All my life I hated my father. I was angry with him for certain things he'd done and attitudes he'd held. Until his death and long after, I'd remained resentful of him and his actions. Recently however something has changed, shifted. Something has come to light that made me realize that for too many years I'd misjudged him, holding a grudge that was, to some extent, unfair. To be frank, I allowed myself to stay stuck in a narrow-minded and fixed mindset.'

I took an old leather wallet that once belonged to my dad from my pocket and retrieved a flaky piece of paper from a compartment where the leather was thinning. Brandon stooped for a closer look as Heather concentrated her flashlight on the fragile paper. Tim sat slightly back, giving them space to see clearly. He'd already seen what I was about to share.

'Back in the house you didn't want to play the gratitude game, seeing it as boring, repetitive and no longer relevant. I think this is an example of you being stuck in a fixed mindset. I've brought you to this log cabin to challenge this so that you don't make the same mistakes I made.'

Brandon looked confused.

'Sit down. Let me tell you the story of this piece of paper. It's the story of a broken heart and begins the day I was born.'

Coffee Time!

As you prepare to read the story I shared with Brandon that day, grab your coffee. Although this story is slightly longer than usual, I believe it will help you begin to explore two crucial questions that we examine more deeply later in the *Sip*.

1: How are you stuck in a *fixed mindset?*
2: How is this detrimental to you stepping into the POWER of your POTENTIAL?

My Broken Heart

'When my great-grandmother first held me, she said, 'There's something wrong with this child. She's breathing too fast. Her heart's too fast.' At the time, no one took any notice of her. However, in 1950 when I was around four months old I was very sick and put on oxygen in an oxygen tent. The doctors couldn't work out if I'd had a heart attack or was suffering from pneumonia. Eventually, when I was well enough, I left the hospital without them ever clarifying exactly what had been wrong with me. Right after that, my parents started taking me to a pediatrician in Columbus who, when I was about three-years old, referred me to Riley Children's Hospital in Indianapolis. The records I have of my time there begin when I was three years old.

Back in the early 1950s, hospitals were very traumatic for children. The quiet waiting room was merely a row of folding chairs, seating anxious parents with nervous children along a hallway outside the examining rooms. Somebody would come and call the child's name and parents weren't allowed to go in with them. So, there I am at three years old, having to walk in to be examined by people that I've never before seen. I can remember the hallway. I remember the chairs clearly. I'm not sure how much I remember about being examined. I do remember finding it very frightening. In all the physicians' notes that I've read relating to the examinations, the doctors had written something to this effect, 'the patient has been very difficult to examine because she was crying all the time.' Or, 'it was hard to get readings because she was screaming.' Well, *yes*, I now think to myself when I read those notes, *of course I was screaming. I was a tiny child who was very frightened who didn't have a clue what was going on and was there alone without my parents. Of course, I was screaming and crying!*

Around that time, Great-Uncle Lowell, who was married to Aunt Florence, took me to the park where he lifted me to the top of a slide so that I could slide down. He told the other children waiting their turn, 'This little girl's very sick. Let's just let her slide down once.' Even at that time, I didn't want to be considered different to any of the other children. I used to think: *Don't tell them that. I'm fine.* In wintertime especially, I was pretty much homebound except for visiting my grandparents, aunts and uncles. Everyone was terrified that I'd become sick.

Over time, many tests were done at Riley Hospital. During these appointments monitors were strapped to my body and endless examinations were conducted. Despite this, they initially found it hard to work out what was wrong with me. My mother told me that for a long time, they thought I had cystic fibrosis, believing my lungs to be the root of the issues. It was a scary time for everyone, especially my parents. If I became the slightest bit sick, or my temperature rose, I had to be taken to the hospital immediately. One day, I'd had enough. I'd been strapped to lots of monitors and had to repeatedly climb up and down four steps. One time, I stomped my foot saying, 'no, I'm not going to do it anymore.' You can imagine me as a stubborn four-or five-year-old! *No! Not doing it!* Of course, everyone was telling me, 'Cindy, you must.' At this point, I got down on the floor and threw a temper tantrum, still with the monitors attached. That was the moment when something shifted for the doctor.

That was the first time they realized that my heart was the problem. To determine the exact diagnosis, I needed a heart catheterization. As I had to be awake during the procedure, the student nurses, who I loved, would read me stories to keep me calm. I remember clearly how this was right before Thanksgiving because there is a photo of your uncle Doug and me dressed to go to Grandma or Aunt Florence's for the celebration. I had a big gauze bandage on my arm in the photo. Eventually, heart surgery was scheduled. Because I suffered a lot with bronchitis a break between bouts was the optimum time for the surgery. Even today, heart surgery is a terrifying prospect. Can you imagine what it was like in the 1950s?'

'I had no idea they could do that kind of operation back then,' said Brandon

'That's right. I was one of the first children in the world to ever have heart surgery. I know now that many of the other children who had similar operations at that time didn't make it.'

'You were pretty lucky,' said Brandon.

'Yes. I have a lot to be grateful for – over seventy years' worth of life that I might never have had. Of course, at the time, I didn't realize or appreciate that. As the doctors and my parents tried to prepare me for the surgery, my reaction was, 'okay, yeah, fine.' I was annoyed. 'I have to go back to the hospital again!' It was a tense time for everyone.

I don't remember anything about the surgery. I don't even remember getting ready for it. I do remember the days afterward. There were no such things as private or semi-private rooms. There were just all of these girls in one room. Each had a curtain they could pull around their bed for privacy during doctor's rounds and family visits. My mom had small gifts for me that she had given to the nurses to pass on as parents were only allowed to visit each Wednesday and Sunday for half an hour. The first time my parents saw me after my surgery they were so shocked by the fact that I had color in my cheeks and lips that they asked if the nurses had put make-up on my face. As visiting hours were so limited and I was only six years old - I really missed my mom. The student nurses were, once again, left to comfort me.

As you can imagine, I looked forward to seeing my parents each visiting day. I knew exactly which days they were due to visit and would wait eagerly by the elevator for them to arrive. There was one day, however, that they were supposed to come yet didn't show up. I stood next to the elevator watching because I knew my mommy was going to come. Mommy didn't show up. When I went to sleep that night, I told the nurses to, 'wake me up when Mommy comes, cuz I know she's going to be here.' Neither she nor my father arrived. I hadn't remembered this at all until one day, years later, during a counseling session. The counselor suggested that I ask my mom why she didn't come that day. Thank God, she was still alive. When I asked her, she started crying.

She explained that the doctors stopped her when she went down the elevator to leave, saying, 'It upsets Cindy so much when you leave that it takes us forever to settle her down. Don't come and everything will be okay.'

My mom replied, 'I need to go and tell her.'
The doctor reassured her, 'We'll tell her.'

'No, I need to.'

They wouldn't let her go back. All those years later, my mom asked, 'Didn't they tell you?' 'I don't know,' I told her. Even if they had, I wouldn't have believed it. I would have believed, *my mom's gonna be here.*

I realize now that while I've been profoundly lucky to have a fully functioning heart for all these years, the actions of the doctor that day to prevent my parents from visiting me had other, not so positive, long-lasting implications. A major issue has been a lifelong fear of abandonment and the other was a long-lasting grudge against my father. I had erroneously considered him to be responsible for preventing my mother from visiting me. This contributed to a very difficult relationship with him that, until I met Tim, spilled over into every adult male relationship I had.

It wasn't until many years later, as my dad was aging, that it came to me to have a heart to heart with him. Until that day, this had been pretty much impossible. I told him that I'd been seeing a counselor and she'd encouraged me to speak to my mom about why they hadn't visited me. When I recounted the conversation with my mom, my dad began to cry. I began to see then how, perhaps, my dad wasn't as guilty as I'd thought. However, I wasn't quite ready to let go of my grudge. Somehow, it helped me to hang on to my anger. When he became too old and frail to use this cabin, I gladly let it fall into ruin. I didn't care when the brambles began to overwhelm it. As he grew closer to death, I also wasn't too concerned with doing anything to improve my relationship with him. Following his death, however, something extraordinary came to light.

While clearing out his belongings, I came across his wallet. As I opened the billfold, I discovered a fragile piece of folded paper, flaky around the edges. I was deeply shocked to see that on it was drawn a picture of my broken heart. It was the piece of paper on which my dad had asked the surgeon to draw a diagram of my heart to help him understand exactly how it was broken and how they were going to mend it. I had no idea that he had kept it so close to him for the rest of his life.

Of course, at that moment in time, I wished he were still alive so that I could thank him. It was then that something crucial shifted for me. I began to realize that I'd been stuck in rigid patterns, thoughts and behaviors with roots from long ago that were no longer truly serving me. Perhaps they'd needlessly contributed to a difficult relationship with my father. This is when I truly began my own journey of shifting from a *fixed mindset to a growth mindset*, using gratitude to help me. Looking back, I realize that I have my father to partly thank for that.

Brandon quietly observes the paper in my hand where the faded diagram of my young heart is visible.

'So that's why the Thanksgiving gratitude game is important to you. You know how easy it is for us to miss opportunities to appreciate and enjoy great gifts in life.'

'Yes. I have every reason to be more grateful than most. I understand how lucky I am and how life is precious. I don't want you, or anyone, to miss opportunities to appreciate the blessings in their life. Aunt Florence did a great job at teaching me this during her life, but it was finding this paper in my father's wallet that truly helped me to fully understand.'

'I get it Mom.'

I could tell by the look in his eyes that he really did understand. I hope you do, too. Can you think of any aspects of your own life where you've allowed closed thinking, a fixed mindset, to keep you small? If so, we need to eradicate that so that you can step fully into your Vital Vision. We do that now as I ask you to:

Tell Me, *How do you Shift from a Fixed to a Growth Mindset?*

Tell Me, How do you Shift from a Fixed to a Growth Mindset?

INTENTIONS

To:

- Define *fixed* and *growth mindset*.
- Explore how you can shift from a *fixed mindset to a growth mindset*.
- Explain how this supports your Vital Vision.

In the last *Sip*, you identified:

- Where, how and why you're showing up as a crew member at a basic level.
- Where, how and why you're showing up as a crew member at a Super Deluxe Delight level.

Tell me, at what level did you honor your *Reflection* focused Shift Action Step this week?

1	2	3	4	5	6	7	8	9	10

What worked for you?   Why?
What didn't work for you?   Why not?
What do you still need to do?

Reflection

The ability to look at your own actions, thoughts, and beliefs with honesty & integrity so that you can show up in life for yourself, and others, at the highest and most enjoyable level.

....

....

....

Tell me, how how did this help to support the overall development of your Vital Vision?

....

....

....

A Year From Now

To begin delving more deeply into this *Sip*, I'd like you to consider this question: A year from now, no matter what you do, you WILL have results in your life, but will they be results that you LOVE?

Top Tip: Passion is not always enough

What you do is built on your passion but no matter how passionate you are, sometimes it isn't enough. This holds true for all people, at all levels, in every walk of life, in every region of the world.

That means it holds true for you.

Your Mindset

As we explored in the last *Sip*, your mindset can get in your way of accomplishing results that you LOVE and cause a negative mood in your head. Your mindset, beliefs and the way you think override everything. It can:

- Filter what you see, hear, think, feel, and do.
- Frame the running account that's taking place in your head.
- Guide the whole interpretation process.

In fact, the biggest and deepest communication gap is between you and your own mind. This communication gap creates a *fixed mindset* where your internal monologue is focused on judging both yourself and others. It keeps you rooted in fear and self-doubt.

Consider these thoughts. Do any resonate with you?

- I'm a loser; I'm not enough.
- Why did they win when I didn't?
- I'm a bad person.
- My partner is selfish.
- I wasn't born with this talent, and I can't learn this.

Beliefs Create Outcome

You may have heard 'your perception is your reality'. It's true. The scenario we tell ourselves is what our mind believes. Our beliefs create our outcomes. Consciously, or subconsciously, we create our circumstances due to our thoughts. It's helpful to remember these three key facts:

1. We're all the product of a state of mind that we held at some point in our life.
2. We don't know how to improve our state of mind.
3. We don't know how to stop old belief tapes in our minds because we don't even know we're creating these thoughts.

The sooner we accept that we're creating these judgmental thoughts, the sooner we can take responsibility for creating an adjustment. Imagine instead being confident and courageous, having belief in yourself and in the right mindset to implement vital, joyful and life enhancing shifts. I'm talking about a *growth mindset*.

The Shift Café Definition of Growth Mindset

A mindset that is constantly open to new levels
of learning, developing and understanding.

With a **Growth Mindset**, you:

- Spend more time looking inside and understanding yourself so that you can stop looking around and harshly judging yourself and others.
- Feel excited when you break through old patterns of thinking and behaving.
- Focus on your unique abilities that will support learning and growth.
- Focus on solving the problem rather than worrying about the size of it.
- Focus on learning and developing.
- Focus on reasons larger than yourself.

People with a *growth mindset* are constantly learning, monitoring and understanding what's going on instead of judging themselves and others. It's helpful to remember that committing to living with this expansive perspective has many benefits that help you to:

- Embrace a love of learning and a flexibility that is essential for you to achieve great results.
- Embrace challenges and failures as opportunities to learn and grow.
- Persist despite setbacks.
- Use new information to adjust thoughts and plans.

With a *growth mindset* you understand that mindset shifts are necessary for creating new habits, seeing challenges as opportunities and learning how to deal with setbacks. Perhaps most importantly you grasp that mindset shifts begin in the heart then branch out in every possible direction. In various situations, people with a growth mindset ask themselves:

- What can I learn from this?
- How can I improve?
- How can I help my partner/friends/family do this better?

You've already seen how that happened with me when I discovered the fragile paper in my father's wallet. I'd now like to share a more recent experience where I had another opportunity to shift from a fixed to a growth mindset. It took place during a recent visit with Brandon and Heather who live on family farmland in Indiana.

A Lesson From the Fireflies

The farm has been in my family for several generations. Heather and Brandon had recently moved there and were in the process of settling in. As my husband Tim and I had been at our home in Arizona for a few months, we hadn't seen them for quite a while. We spent a lovely afternoon catching up over drinks and my favorite strawberry shortcake. Later, as dusk drew in, Heather suggested that we move to the garden to watch the fireflies. I have to be honest, I didn't initially see the great attraction. I was comfortable doing what generations of my family had always done on the farm, which is to sit around the kitchen table and chat. However, I followed Heather into the garden where, as night fell, we became surrounded by the glimmering light of thousands of tiny insects. I was filled with a sense of wonder. How had I never experienced this on the farm before? All it had taken was for Heather to shift us, and for me to be willing to shift with her, from our habitual seats inside the house to the garden for a precious new memory to be created. I learned a lot from Heather that day about being open to new experiences in environments where my habits and expectations had become unconsciously rigid and entrenched. Did you notice the word habitual? Many sabotaging thoughts, feelings and actions are simply ingrained habits that create, or have roots in, a *fixed mindset*.

Coffee Time!

Grab your coffee! It's time to reflect on your own sabotaging habits so that you can begin the process of shifting from *a fixed mindset to a growth mindset*. I admit that for some *fixed mindset* obstacles it's not going to be simple. Some require deeper work. As you're at the beginning of your shift journey, let's begin with your most obvious obstacles. Remember how, in the *Sip 5*, you identified potential success sabotaging thoughts, feelings or actions in relation to attaining your Vital Vision? Remind yourself of them by listing your top three below:

Three of my potential success sabotaging thoughts, feeling or actions are:

1.

2.

3.

Golden Obstacles (GO)

What if you were able to shift your *fixed mindset* as simply as I shifted from my comfortable seat in my daughter-in-law's kitchen to the garden? I believe you can! Whenever you step into a new challenge, such as attaining your Vital Vision, blocks may arise that shape your confidence. You may believe that you'll never attain success. Some of the most common obstacles are discussed in the *Between the Sips* section of this book. However, here at *The Shift Café*, we believe that becoming aware of these blocks turns them into *Golden Obstacles*. Why? Once you're aware of them and how they negatively impact your well-being, you can work to release them. This helps you to travel further along your path to success, which leads to powerful shifts and breakthroughs.

How Do I Shift From a Fixed Mindset to a Growth Mindset?

Let's explore the following six steps to help you shift from a *fixed mindset* to a *growth mindset*. To begin, I'd like to give you some good news! You've already completed the first step! Take a look.

Step 1. Define your current state.

In a previous *Sip*, I asked you, 'What is causing you to feel overwhelmed, unfulfilled or stuck?' That helps determine your current state – where you want to shift from. Take a moment to remember what you said, make a note here:

-
-
-

Step 2. Create Your Vital Vision.

Did you notice? You've already created this step too! Has anything shifted with your Vital Vision? Often, by this stage, you might notice elements that don't feel quite right, need adjusting or even releasing. Can you clarify, refine or re-define your Vital Vision? Take a moment to write a new, laser sharp, version of your Vital Vision.

My laser sharp Vital Vision is:

....

....

....

....

....

....

Step 3. Listen to your inner critic that judges you and others.

Is it saying:

- What if I disappoint others?
- It's not my fault. It was something or someone else's fault.
- What if I fail? People will laugh at me.
- Why do they get to do it instead of me?
- It's impossible to do this.

Step 4. Empower Yourself. Shift from, I don't have any options to I always have options.

You can choose to interpret challenges from a fixed mindset where you're continuously judging, blaming and playing old negative and destructive tapes or you can choose to interpret them from a growth mindset. It's up to you. Why not give grace to yourself and others?

Step 5. Change your Language.

As you approach a challenge, think about the language you choose to use: '

Fixed Mindset	Growth Mindset
I'm not good at this.	I'm not sure I can do it **yet**, but I can learn.
It's not my fault, it's your fault.	If I don't take responsibility, I can't fix it. Let me listen & learn.
I know I'm going to fail.	All successful people had failure along the way. What can I learn from them?
If only I had more money.	What do I need to do differently? Who can I talk to learn?

Step 6. Take action steps towards your Vital Vision.

Over time, you get to choose whether you:

- Take on the challenge wholeheartedly.
- Learn from your setbacks and try again.
- Hear, and act on, any criticism.

To help you shift firmly into the growth mindset, it's helpful to identify an action that you can take that will help you keep track of your success and move you closer to your Vital Vision. Like most people, I've had difficult times where my thoughts have told me that I'm not good enough, and I still go there sometimes. I've learned, however, how and when to shift my mindset from *fixed to growth.* Let me give you an example of how, in my professional role, I used the *Six Steps to Shift from a Fixed Mindset to a Growth Mindset.*

Six Steps to Shift from a Fixed Mindset to a Growth Mindset.

I once worked with a vice president of a manufacturing company who told me that he wanted to terminate the contract of an employee. I told him that I would investigate this employee's performance reviews, coaching comments and then get back with him. However, the following day, the VP saw this employee within the building. Storming into my office, he expressed his anger that this employee had not yet been informed of the termination of his contract. Pacing the floor, he yelled and gesticulated aggressively at me. In the past, I would have reacted from my *fixed mindset* — judging him, listening to my old tapes. Instead, I utilized the *Six Steps of Shifting from a Fixed Mindset to a Growth Mindset:*

1st Step: Defined my Current State

> I quietly identified that I was feeling shocked and outraged with this VP while he stomped around my office.

2nd Step: Created My Vital Vision

> I visualize myself standing up to the VP, refusing to be intimidated or acting unethically in my work.

3rd Step: Listened to my inner critic that judges others and me.

It was saying:
'Cindy, you don't have to put up with this—fight back.'
It was, however, also saying:
'Maybe it's better to just do what he wants.'

4th Step: Empowered myself, shifting from thoughts of I don't have any options to I always have options.

I told myself:

'I can choose how I react; I know I'm following
the correct contract termination process and
I refuse to lower myself to his level.'
I asked myself, 'Why is he acting like this?'

5th Step: Changed my language.

- I said to myself: 'Cindy, imagine you have a bullet-proof glass between you & him so that no matter what he says, you will not allow it to get to you.'
- I also said to myself 'You need to relax your shoulders, maintain eye contact—but don't show that you are upset. Take a drink of your coffee.'

6th Step: Chose, and took, Shift Action Steps toward my Vital Vision.

> - I put up my bullet-proof glass, made sure to breathe normally, stayed relaxed and even took a drink of my coffee.
> - Importantly – I didn't just react.

Your Turn!

You've heard my story. It's now your turn to prepare for your shift from a *fixed mindset to growth mindset*. Thinking about your Vital Vision and the top three golden obstacles you've just identified, complete the following table answering these questions:

- What is the *fixed mindset* behind each of your *Golden Obstacles* (GO)?
- How can you shift that to a *growth mindset*?
- What action are you going to take to ensure/reinforce the *growth mindset*?

In the table below, list your top three *Golden Obstacles*. Then, write down how this can shift to a *growth mindset*. Then decide, and make note of, the *Growth Action Step* that will ensure you shift from a *fixed to growth mindset*.

Fixed Mindset	Growth Mindset	Growth Mindset Action
GO1:		
GO2:		
GO3:		

Congratulations! You have now got a clear idea of how to shift your *fixed mindset* into a *growth mindset* and which growth mindset actions that will help you take the required steps to attain your Vital Vision!

7-Day Level 10 Growth Mindset Shift Challenge!

For the next seven days, commit to practicing your *Growth Mindset* Action at a Level 10. Take a few moments each day to reflect and journal on any *Golden Obstacles* you come across. Tracking and honoring these will fuel energy for greater mindset shifts. You could even reflect on how these shifts relate to your Legacy Influencer. How could they influence your new *growth mindset?* I know these are difficult topics but in order to live your life at your highest level, you will meet mindset challenges along the way. The more lucid you become about obstacles, the more shifts you'll be able to make. You just need to keep repeating the *Six Steps to Shifting from a Fixed Mindset to a Growth Mindset.*

Golden Obstacles
Journal on your *Golden Obstacles* in the space below:

Nurturing Growth Mindset – Vital Vision
Shift Action Step

Your beliefs that affect how you choose to think, feel, and react to any situation.

Tell me, what *Growth Mindset* focused Vital Vision Shift Action Step will you take this week?

....

....

....

Your mindset can get in your way of accomplishing results that you LOVE.

Tell me, at what level are you going to honor your *Growth Mindset* focused Shift Action Step this week?

| 1 | 2 | 3 | 4 | 5 | 6 | 7 | 8 | 9 | 10 |

Uproot fear and self-doubt.

Tell me, how will this support the successful attainment of your Vital Vision?

....

....

....

The more lucid you become about obstacles, the more shifts you'll be able to make.

Serenity Basket Heart Wisdom
Reflect on this question:

From what I've learned today, does my heart have any further wisdom that will help me to attain my Vital Vision?

....

....

....

Place this guidance into your Serenity Basket. Let it help you on your journey through The Shift Café.

Congratulations! In this *Sip*, you have:
- Defined Fixed and Growth Mindset.
- Explored how you can shift from a Fixed Mindset to a Growth Mindset.
- Understood how this helps your Vital Vision

Remember:

> *Shifts begin in the heart — then branch out in every direction.*

In the next *Sip*, I'll show how becoming clear on your values creates a strong foundation for successful shifts to happen. I ask: **Tell Me**, What are Your Values? See you there!

Ode To Spring

by Teo Eve

when your solitary herald flower

'fans to a forest glade of 'cissus

and emeralds blaze the muddied
grasses, tourmaline shimmers in
a glaze of dew;

you split the globe's face to a
sunny smile, butter barren ground
with golden glows, stud verdant
stones in winter's crown
and sap snow-trenches with all the urgency

of April showers; untangling frozen webs
that silked our months in captive spiras, kick
starting summer-sands of time. And though
beyond these mountains green we know
your rain-reprise of

flowered buds lasts but a mayfly
hour, and summer's seas sap away
these sands of mine, we still go to
the woodland bower
where evergreens in ignorance twirl, basking
in your eternal hour.

#2 O = Overwhelm

Life can be demanding. We often juggle being a partner and/or parent alongside demanding careers. Additionally, we manage domestic and financial responsibilities. You might even be caring for grandchildren or aging parents. Somewhere in this mix, you squeeze in friends and a social life. While it can be exciting to have a full schedule, it can also, sometimes, feel overwhelming.

The Shift Café Definition of Overwhelm

To feel buried under, and unable to cope
with, the multiple demands of life.

The Impact of Overwhelm

I often hear the following comments during The Shift Café conversations from participants who are having problems stepping fully into their Vital Vision:

- My days are tightly scheduled.
- I can't keep up this pace.
- I have no me time.
- My life is wearing me out.
- I can't make important decisions.

Slow Down

At times, everyone feels overwhelmed by a lack of time, too many expectations and responsibilities. It's a natural response to having too many things going on at once and is your body's way of telling you that you need to slow down. Realize this: it's your body's way of helping you.

Thinking and Overwhelm

Feeling overwhelmed is more than having too much to do. It's often also about having too much to think about. Our brains are capable of juggling an amazing amount of information. You may, however, eventually reach overload and begin losing things, avoiding people and events, find yourself becoming angry or struggling in all areas of your life. The best way to deal with feeling overwhelmed is to get past all the thinking and take action.

Take Action with The 4 Ns

In The Shift Café, we believe that it's helpful for you to have tools, in addition to checklists, schedules, and prioritizing, to work through your feelings of being overwhelmed. Allow me to share four tools, the **4 Ns,** that have worked for me and many of my Shift Café participants.

N1: Name It

Describe your feelings of overwhelm using feeling words and phrases, such as:

I feel ....
I am noticing...
I acknowledge a feeling(s) of...

Naming the emotion doesn't add fire to the flame as some fear. It smothers and calms it. Once you name what you're feeling, you can start taming it. You'll notice how you become less engulfed and able to move forward.

N2: Connect with **Nature.**

By now you know that here at The Shift Café, we value time in nature. Why? Exposure to nature not only makes you feel better emotionally, it also contributes to your physical well-being. Spending as little as two minutes outdoors allows you to:

Slow down
Be present in the moment
Focus 100% of your energy on the birds, plants, trees, and animals.

Tuning in with your senses, what you can see, hear, smell, feel or touch allows you to connect with something greater than yourself. If you can't go outside, look out a window or focus on a beautiful photo or painting of nature.

N3: Do the **Next** Right Thing

Focus on the very next step that is right for you — not for someone else. Ask yourself:

'What is the very next right step that I now need to take?'

Focus on actions to help you grow. This helps you make simple and achievable choices that are best for you in each moment rather than maintaining focus on the many things you believe you should be doing. Repeat this question each time you feel overwhelmed. It will help you move forward.

N4. Say **No** to Yourself and Others.

First: Say 'No' to Yourself
Can you really multitask, i.e. perform more than one task at the same time?

No

Multitasking is a myth. I've tried it and didn't finish anything! Our brain cannot switch back and forth between tasks that are complex and require our active attention. When you rapidly switch from one task to another you exhaust your brain causing delays and loss of focus. Say 'no' to multitasking so that you can focus on completing one task at a time.

Second: Say 'No' to Others.

You have only so much time and energy to get your wants and needs met. Constantly saying 'yes' to others prioritizes their wants and needs over yours thus leaving you feeling more overwhelmed. The word 'no' has power. Practice saying these sentences without apologizing.

No, thank you.

No, thank you. I won't be able to.

Thank you for asking me, but that's not going to work for me.

My calendar is full.

Coffee Time!

Tell me, what is currently causing you to feel overwhelmed?

....

....

....

Tell me, how do you currently deal with feeling overwhelmed?

....

....

....

Tell me, how could using the **4Ns** change your feelings towards being overwhelmed?

....

....

....

Nurturing the 4Ns- Vital Vision Shift Step

Overwhelm

To feel buried under, and unable to cope with, the multiple demands of life.

The 4Ns

Tools to help you work through feelings of overwhelm.

Tell me, what three actions will you take the next time you are feeling overwhelmed?

Dwelling on feelings of over-whelm and letting them knock you off course can be detrimental to both you and others.

1.

2.

3.

Remember:

Naming the emotion doesn't add fire to the flame as some might fear.

It smothers and calms it.

We now return to your next Sip where we will gather in The Shift Café forest where I invite you to: **Tell Me**, What are Your Values? See you there!

The Shift Café
Nurturing your wisdom, intelligence, beauty and spirit — one sip at a time.

Contemplation Nook

Sip 9
Nurturing Values

*A man who dares to waste one hour of time has
not discovered the value of life.*

Charles Darwin

The Shift Café Definition of Values

A meaningful set of rules guiding life choices

Thanksgiving Evening
The Cabin in the Forest

As I finished my tale, everyone remained lost in thought. The fragile paper rested in my hands like a broken winged butterfly. With Bailey close at his heel, Tim lit a fire to alleviate the icy cold of the cabin.

'May I?' Brandon held out his hand.

Not convinced I wanted to share this delicate fragment of paper that had become so precious to me, I hesitated. Tim threw me an encouraging glance. I knew what he thought I should do.

After gently placing the wafer thin paper into Brandon's hands, he inspected what had been carried for many years close to the heart of his grandfather. I couldn't help noticing the manliness of his hands. Memories of holding them when he was a small boy fused with memories of other times. Tim and I taking him on camping trips; my dad's stern face; Aunt Florence taking Brandon on a butterscotch pie hunt; my mother telling me about her friends at work; the day she and my father didn't visit me in the hospital; my terror; the fear of that little girl — so young and so alone.

'For all those years, I'd hated my dad, blaming him for abandoning me. Yet, here I am, almost sixty-five years later, finally comprehending how wrong I'd been. I had completely misjudged my father's values. I'd thought of my dad as being nothing but cruel yet he had actually been holding my best interests at heart. He put my life first, over his own fears. He even ignored the advice of his mother who was carrying her own fears from the loss of her son. He put my life — my survival — over his painful memories of his brother's death. He knew that if the operation was not a success, I could die. Yet, he placed his trust in those pioneering surgeons. I came to realize that in order to do this he must've loved me deeply. Ultimately, his love for me was greater than his fear.

My feelings towards my dad changed. I realized that somewhere deep inside, in those early days of my childhood, he had very strong values, especially in relation to family. This was proven to me by this piece of flaky paper. For the rest of his life, my father carried a picture of my heart close to his own.'

'Mom, this is an incredible story,' said Brandon, returning the paper. 'What are you going to do with it?'

Until that moment, it hadn't occurred to me to do anything with it. As flames from the fire gently warmed the cabin, Brandon's question gave me a nudge, showing me what I needed to do.

'I'm going to tell it. In doing so, I hope I can help others take the time to reflect on, and evaluate, the old grudges they're holding onto that are no longer needed so that they can let them go. I want them to explore who they are without fixed mindsets burdening them. This way, they'll come to a fresh place where they can begin to examine what is now truly important to them. Not by holding on to the past, but by looking forwards to a high quality future. In order for them to attain this, I want to help them become clear on their values.'

And so, sitting before the fire in my father's old cabin in the midst of the forest thicket surrounded by those I love the most, my clarity for the Vital Vision of this book expanded. The power of this story, my life experiences and the potential my

story has to encourage others to release obstacles and grudges became clear to me. I hope you can see how it can help you.

In bringing this book to life, one of the things I've drawn on deeply is my faith in my life values. I believe that for your Vital Vision to blossom, you need to be super clear on your values, yet so many people aren't. Therefore, in today's Sip, I ask you:

Tell Me, What Are Your Values?

Tell Me, What are Your Values?

> ### INTENTIONS
>
> ~⚬~✿~⚬~✿~⚬~✿~⚬~
>
> **To:**
> - Identify Your Life Values.
> - Clarify how you can honor them so that they support your Vital Vision.

In the last *Sip* you:

- Defined fixed and growth mindset.
- Explored how you can shift from a fixed mindset to a growth mindset.
- Understood how this helps your Vital Vision.

Tell me, at what level did you honor your Growth Mindset Shift Action Step this week?

1   2   3   4   5   6   7   8   9   10

What worked for you?   Why?
What didn't work for you?   Why not?
What do you still need to do?

Mindset

Your beliefs that affect how you choose to think, feel, and react to any situation.

....

....

....

Tell me, did this help to support the overall development of your Vital Vision?

....

....

....

Values

The steps that you take today, and the thoughts that you think, are going to affect tomorrow. Not only is it important to have a clear idea of what you want your life to look like, it's also important to understand how your Vital Vision aligns with the values for how you live your life. Clarity about your values will help you create a clear road map, with healthy and happy boundaries, that will aid the success of attaining your Vital Vision.

Many of my workshop participants and clients don't know their core values in life. This makes it harder for them to achieve their goals, as they don't understand the reasons behind wanting them. In this Sip, you will work out your core values for your life in general and, specifically, for your Vital Vision.

Define Your Values

When I first identified my values twenty years ago, I discovered that four core values governed my life:

1. Spirituality
2. Family
3. Integrity
4. Relationships

For each of these, I created a statement:

Spiritual: I believe that a Higher Power is in control of my life. I must have faith and let go.

Family: I listen to my family and support them unconditionally. They are also my support.

Integrity: In every situation, I am honest and ethical. I will only be involved in honest and ethical activities.

Relationships: I nurture my relationships with family, friends, co-workers and clients.

Intention

To ensure that I was honoring each of these, I gave each of them an intention that would help me understand why they were important to me.

Spiritual: To consciously develop a more intimate relationship with a Higher Being.

Family: To regularly schedule quality time with individual family members in order to share and hear how they are and what they need.

Integrity: To research any activities and organizations, including the leaders attached to them, that I'm interested in supporting. I want to ensure they are operating from an ethical and honest stance.

Relationships: To consciously focus on regular acts of care towards my family, friends, co-workers and clients.

Becoming clear on these values helped me to maintain a steady hand on the steering wheel of all aspects and new projects in my life, including creating this book.

A Word of Warning — Not All Values are Equal!

It's important to remember that your values are personal to you. What you define as family may be different to my definition of family. How you understand spirituality may contrast with my views on spirituality. When you place one value higher on the list than another person has placed it, it does not mean that the position of their value is any less important than your positioning. There are no rights or wrongs. There is no superiority or inferiority.

Understanding the Role (and value!) of Values — your why.

Sometimes, my clients surprise me with the values they determine for themselves. Sophie is a devoted single mother to her teenage daughter and a freelance writer. From the outside, I could see that most of her time was taken with supporting her daughter, including having put aspects of her professional, domestic, financial and romantic life on hold in order to give her daughter her full focus. She is also a person who values her relationship with spirituality. Imagine my surprise when she defined her core values as:

1. Professionalism
2. Efficiency
3. Success

These were not visibly apparent in her everyday life. I had fully expected family and spirituality to top her list. Wanting to understand more clearly, I asked her,

'Tell Me, why have you placed these at the top?'

'By ensuring that I'm working at a high professional and efficient standard, I can create the success that I need to ensure that my daughter is well cared and provided for,' she said.

Even though she hadn't named family as her priority, it became clear that her why behind her values formed an integral part of her value base. Interestingly, with each piece of work that Sophie took on she not only ensured that it honored her values but also fit around her daughter's needs.

Now grab your coffee as we head into Coffee Time where you'll begin to explore your own values.

Coffee Time!

Having taken Bailey outside for a short walk, Heather returned with a bunch of damp fall leaves retrieved from the snow. They were as fragile as my father's paper. after drying them before the fire, I handed some to each of them. 'Tell me,' I asked, 'if these were to represent your values, what would each leaf represent?' If you'd been with us, I wonder what your leaf, or leaves, might represent for you. Let's explore.

Identifying Your Life Values and Why They're Important to You.

If you're new to understanding, identifying and clarifying your values, it can be hard to work out exactly what they are. I encourage my clients and workshop participants to begin with a *Don't Mess with ....* list.

The Shift Café Definition of *Don't Mess With...*

Your hard line in the sand that
no one is allowed to cross.

Most people can easily think of things for this list. For example:

- Don't mess with my children/parents/partner.
- Don't mess with my dog/cat/horse/pet.

Tell me, what's on your *Don't Mess With* ... list? Journal as many as you can then write the top three below...

1: *Don't Mess with.....*

2: *Don't Mess with.....*

3: *Don't Mess with....*

Value Statement

Now turn each of your *Don't Mess With* ... statements into value statements.

For example:

Don't mess with my daughter
becomes:
I always protect my daughter.

Tell me, what are your value statements based on your *Don't Mess With* beliefs?

-
-
-

Clarifying Your Why

Sophie's primary *Don't Mess with* ... value was:

Don't Mess with ..... my professionalism

Sophie's Why Statements

I value my professionalism for two reasons:

1. It ensures that I work in such a way to be able to provide well for my daughter.

2. Honoring and protecting my professionalism ensures that I get quality time with my daughter. This is the most precious thing in the world to me.

Tell me, what are your why statements based on your '*Don't Mess With ...*' beliefs?

-

-

-

-

Setting the Intention — Honoring Your Values.

How are you going to respect your values? It's important that you do respect them because if you don't, no one else will. To help you protect your values, and the why behind them, it's helpful to create a simple and easy intention that reminds you why the value is important to you. Knowing this will help you respect it. Remember my clarifying statements above? Here's a reminder:

Family: I listen to my family; support them unconditionally. They are also my support.

Tell me, what are your clarifying statements for each of your value statements:

-

-

-

-

Tell me, how do these values and intentions align with your Vital Vision?

Can you see a clear correlation between your life values and intentions and your Vital Vision? If not, take a few moments to see if you need to tweak anything. Once you feel you have alignment with your life values and Vital Vision, write a paragraph to claim it.

My life values are:

....

....

....

They support my Vital Vision by:

....

....

....

I honor them by:

....

....

....

Long into the evening we sat clutching our leaves before the fire in my father's cabin. Each of us reflected on the story of my heart and how it would now impact our life values. Heather, a huge animal lover, decided she wanted to commit more strongly to protecting the animals of the farmland. Brandon would commit more fully to his care for local politics. Tim and I decided to ensure that we would spend more quality time with each other.

'You know, Mom,' said Brandon, 'I'll always feel grateful for this night.'

'Me too,' I replied.

'Tell me,' I asked him, 'will you moan about playing the gratitude game next Thanksgiving?'

'No!'

I could tell by the look in his eyes that he meant it. I'm glad I took them all to the cabin in the forest.

The Shift Café Sketching Corner
Value Leaves

Take a moment to draw a leaf or leaves that represent your values.
Label each one with notes on your:
- *'Don't Mess with ...'* statement
- Value Statement
- Your why

Place this picture in your Serenity Basket.
Let the wisdom on each leaf support your Shift Café Journey.

Nurturing Values – Vital Vision Shift Action Step

Values

*A meaningful
set of rules
guiding life
choices.*

Tell me, what *Values* focused Vital Vision Shift Action Step will you take this week?

....

....

*Don't mess
with ....*

....

Tell me, at what level are you going to honor your *Values* focused
Vital Vision Shift Action Step this week?

*The steps you
take today,
and the
thoughts that
you think, are
going to affect
tomorrow.*

1   2   3   4   5   6   7   8   9   10

Tell me, will this support the successful attainment of your
Vital Vision?

*Clarity about
your values will
help you create a
clear road map,
with healthy
and happy
boundaries.*

....

....

....

Serenity Basket Heart Wisdom

Reflect on this question:

From what I've learned today, does my heart have any further wisdom that will help me to attain my Vital Vision?

....

....

....

Place this guidance into your Serenity Basket. Let it help you on your journey through *The Shift Café*.

Congratulations! In this *Sip*, you have:

- Identified Your Life Values.
- Clarified how you can honor them so that they support your Vital Vision.

Remember:

> *Understanding your life values will provide a foundation of clarity.*

Now that you've identified your values, in the next *Sip*, we're going to explore how to set boundaries so that that no one is able to dishonor them. I ask you: **Tell Me**, What are Your Boundaries?

See you there!

Spirit

By Andrew Roberts

1: I am the Rain,

I am the Sunshine,

I am the soft whispering Breeze,

The energy of the Trees,

I am your future

and your past,

I am here,

I never go away,

I am hope on a

lonely day.

2: I am the Shadow

upon your wall,

I am the Ink

that writes the Poem,

I am the sweet

verse of Love,

The Angel from above.

3: I am the face upon

the old photograph,

Your reflection

upon the Lake,

I create stories

Within your Dream,

I am the Rainbow over

The Stream,

I am the Fish of the River,

The Dolphin of the Sea,

I am that Birds the eternally fly Free,

4: I listen to you,

all I ask

is will You listen

to Me?

Contemplation Nook

Sip 10
Nurturing Boundaries

It is not that we are given a short life but we make it short, and we are not
ill-supplied but wasteful of it.

Seneca

The Shift Café Definition of Boundary:

A clear-cut line (boundary line) around your
Vital Vision Values that you don't cross.
Nor do you allow others to cross them.

The Lake
Dawn

We leave the cabin in the magical midnight hours clutching our Value Leaves. Brandon and Heather return to their farm. Tim and I make our way homewards passing Vital Vision Lake where we see silhouettes of both swans sleeping, heads tucked under wings. We are tired yet our hearts are full. I'd like you to imagine that you're following your own path along the lakeshore having exited the forest. Images of fireflies, fires and swans dance around you as you tuck your leaves safely into your Serenity Basket. Although it is still night and you are alone in the forest you feel peaceful. Identifying your values has brought you to a place of inner calm and confidence. You come to the lake shore where, as night turns to dawn, you idly gather twigs and sticks that catch your attention. Then, lulled by the gentle lapping of soft waves, you come to rest on a rock. Worries rise.

What if I can't honor my values?

What if I don't attain my Vital Vision because my values are disrespected?

It's true. It can be hard to respect your values. As we know from the story of my move from the lake house, we all have the potential to sabotage our success and happiness. There are several ways in which we can help ourselves when we are in danger of letting our values be disrespected. We'll explore them in this Sip as I ask you:

Tell Me, What are Your Vital Vision Boundaries?

Tell Me, What Are Your Your Vital Vision Boundaries?

INTENTIONS

- To understand the definition, and importance, of a Vital Vision Boundary.
- To explore how you can create and honor boundaries to support your Vital Vision Values.
- To reflect on how you, and others, respect or disrespect your boundaries.

In the last *Sip*, you:

Values

- Identified Your Values.
- Clarified how you can honor them so that they support your Vital Vision.

A meaningful set of rules guiding life choices.

Remind me: what was your *Values* focused Shift Action Step for the last week?

....

....

....

Tell me, at what level did you implement your *Values* focused Shift Action Step this week?

1   2   3   4   5   6   7   8   9   10

What worked for you?   Why?
What didn't work for you?   Why not?
What do you still need to do?

....

....

....

Tell me, how did this help to support the overall development of your Vital Vision?

....

....

....

Now, let's turn our attention to this week's theme: Vital Vision Boundaries.

Vital Vision Boundaries

Sometimes, it can be tricky to ensure that you, and others, consistently honor your Vital Vision Values. **Tell me**, why do you think it's important to have clear Vital Vision Boundaries to protect your Vital Vision Values?

....

....

....

How Boundaries Protect Your Vital Vision Values
Jasmine's Story

Jasmine was a member of a Shift Café workshop. On the top of her 'Don't mess with my ...' Vital Values list, she'd written:

Don't mess with my son and daughter-in-law.

She had the opportunity to test out this value during a telephone conversation with Laura, a good family friend. Having recently argued with Chloe, Jasmine's daughter-in-law, Laura attempted to share malicious gossip about her. Jasmine's clarity around her *Don't Mess with* My ... values meant that she was able to easily stop the gossiping friend. Calmly, drawing a clear boundary line around her value, Jasmine stated:

'I'm not going to discuss my daughter-in-law with you.'

Disrespecting Boundaries — Be Warned!

When you enforce a boundary with someone for the first time, they're often so shocked or angered that they'll up their game and push against your request. Your job, as someone committed to honoring and respecting your values and boundaries is to stand, as Jasmine did, firmly in your truth.

Accepting the Consequences

Shocked by Jasmine's response, Laura continuously refused to respect Jasmine's boundary. In fact, she escalated her toxicity by suggesting additional horrific behaviors of the daughter-in-law. Jasmine remained firm. Laura attempted several more times to violate Jasmine's boundary. As a result of this continued disrespect, Jasmine ended the friendship. While this was sad for Jasmine, she was resolute. She simply would not break her *Don't Mess with my son or daughter-in-law* boundary — and was prepared to accept the consequences.

Trust Your Instincts
The bonus of understanding and honoring your boundaries.

In order to create, honor and protect your boundaries, you must trust your own instincts. I was once fortunate to be able to travel with my work company to Slovenia in Europe. Prior to the business meeting, my husband, son and I took a magical ten-day trip to Italy. At the end of the trip, they returned home while I traveled on to the meeting. However, as I was on the plane, a sensation rippled through my body and I somehow knew that my life had changed. Later, while sitting in the meeting that felt endlessly tedious, a thought came to me:

Cindy, you need to quit this job.

Flying home, I watched four movies back-to-back and cried because two of the films were set in Italy. I'm sure the person beside me thought that someone had died and, in a way, they were correct. I pulled up the notes section on my phone and wrote:

Italy Trip

This trip was a life changing experience. I've been profoundly emotional all week.

Why?
I feel homesick for what we (my husband, son and I) had last week — time together and fun

In that moment, it became clear how vital my values relating to quality time with family were to my overall well-being. It also became clear that I had not set a firm boundary in my working life to honor this value. My work life, despite being a highly paid and secure corporate job, was drawing me far away from my core family value. I bravely took the decision to honor my instincts by respecting my values and creating clear boundaries. I resigned from my job and have never regretted that decision. Of course, however, before you can respect your boundaries, you have to know what they are. Grab your coffee! Let's explore.

Coffee Time!

Respecting and Disrespecting your Boundaries– A Reflection

Respecting Your Own Boundaries

Tell me, can you recall when you respected your own boundaries?
Think about:

- Your memories of the event/experience?
- What was it?
- How did it feel?
- What happened, or didn't happen, because of you honoring and trusting your own boundaries?

....

....

....

....

....

....

....

....

Disrespecting Your Own Boundaries

Tell me, can you recall a time when you disrespected your own boundaries?
Think about:
- Your memories of the event/experience?
- What was it?
- How did it feel?
- What happened, or didn't happen, because of you not honoring and trusting your boundaries?
- Is there anything you would now do or say differently?

....

....

....

....

When Did Others Respect Your Boundaries

Tell me, can you recall a time when others disrespected your boundaries?
Think about:

- Your memories of the event/experience?
- What was it?
- How did it feel?
- What happened, or didn't happen, because of others honoring and trusting your boundaries?

....

....

....

....

When Did Others Disrespect Your Boundaries

Tell me, can you recall a time when other disrespected your boundaries? Think about:

- Your memories of the event/experience?
- What was it?
- How did it feel?
- What happened, or didn't happen, because of others not honoring and trusting your boundaries?
- Is there anything you would now do or say differently?

....

....

....

....

....

Tell me, what Vital Vision Boundaries do you need so that your Vital Vision Values can be supported?

-

-

-

Bring your attention to the horizon of the lake, the boundary line from which the first light of the day is raising. Admire the stunning colors. Notice how defining your boundaries gives you the confidence to now be able to love yourself, your life and others with confidence and clarity. Each time I walk beside this lake, I come closer to truthfully knowing, honouring and loving myself.

It has been a fruitful day.

The Shift Café Sketching Corner
What Are Your Boundaries?

Sketch the dawn rising over Vital Vision Lake. Which aspect of the lake at dawn represents your Vital Vision Boundaries? Make notes.

Place this picture in your Serenity Basket.
Let the wisdom on each new sunray support your boundaries on your
Shift Café Journey.

Nurturing Boundaries – Vital Vision Shift Action Step

Boundary

*A clear-cut line
(boundary line)
around your
Vital Vision
Values that you
don't cross.
receive this love.*

Tell me, what *Boundary* focused Vital Vision Shift Action Step will you take this week?

....

....

....

*Stand firmly
in
your truth.*

Tell me, at what level are you going to honor your *Boundary* focused Shift Action Step in the coming week?

*Listen to
your
instincts*

$$1 \quad 2 \quad 3 \quad 4 \quad 5 \quad 6 \quad 7 \quad 8 \quad 9 \quad 10$$

Tell me, how will this support the successful attainment of your Vital Vision?

....

....

....

*Trust
yourself*

Serenity Basket Heart Wisdom
Reflect on this question:

From what I've learned today, does my heart have any further wisdom that will help me to attain my Vital Vision?

....

....

....

Place this guidance into your Serenity Basket. Let it help you on your journey through *The Shift Café*.

Congratulations! In this *Sip*, you have:

- Examined the definition, and importance, of a Vital Vision Boundary.
- Explored how you can create, and honor, boundaries to support your Vital Vision Values.
- Reflected on how you, and others, respect or disrespect your boundaries.

Remember:

Boundaries will help you protect your values and
keep your pathway to your Vital Vision clear.

In the next *Sip*, we explore boundaries in more depth as I ask you to: **Tell Me, Are You Able to Take Responsibility?** See You There!

Morn (Dawn)

by Teo Eve

winter bequeathed time
new meaning, broken dawn a slight
prelude to spring's symphony,
amongst minor keys.

april, always, fools
us, teases summer amidst her storms
which pierce these moody shores. a slap
of sea wakens us to seasoned dusk.

celebrity marriage of
morn and night waiting on its quick divorce,
sudden kiss suspending time before swift
partening, as 'all that's best of dark and bright'
lasts a moment in startled eyes: dawn, lifetime,
then the curtain's drawn.

Contemplation Nook

Sip 11

Nurturing Responsibility

The responsibility is all yours; no one can stop you from being honest or straightforward.

Marcus Aurelius

The Shift Café Definition of Responsibility:

❦ ❧ ❦ ❦ ❦ ❧ ❦

Responsibility is:

- The act of being able to accept when you have made a mistake.
- The courage to let go of unhelpful aspects from the past.
- The willingness to make amends and shift thoughts and behavior.

Vital Vision Lake. Release Falls & Herons at Sunrise

You gather your sticks and meander back along the lakeshore until you come to the base of Release Falls. Plummeting from the summit of Vital Vision Hill, it crashes into the main body of the lake. Cool droplets of water ricochet from the water's surface, magnifying sunlight into the day. Removing your shoes, you dip your toes into the water's edge enjoying the sensation of the ice-cold water.

On the far shore, a heron stands stock-still, alert to you and the potential fish it's looking to catch. You eye each other, uncertain. You're in her territory and know you need to respect this. It's your responsibility to think of her needs — what allows her to survive. Equally, you sense that taking responsibility is a vital component of your own survival and potential to turn your life into a success, especially the success of your Vital Vision. To do this, it's important to understand your boundaries and values in relation to how you respect yourself and how others treat you. It's also helpful to examine how you respect the boundaries of others. Additionally it can be crucial to explore how you take responsibility when you make mistakes. Therefore, in today's Sip, I ask you:

Tell Me, Are You Able to Take Responsibility?

Tell Me, Are You Able To Take Responsibility?

INTENTION

To understand how facing up to past mistakes, and being
willing to make amends, can support the success
of your Vital Vision.

In the last *Sip,* you:

Boundary

- Examined the definition, and importance, of a Vital Vision Boundary.

  A clear-cut line
- Explored how you can create, and honor, boundaries to *(boundary line)* support your Vital Vision Values. *around your Vital Vision Values that*
- Reflected on how you, and others, respect or disrespect *you don't cross.* your boundaries.

Remind me, what was your *Boundary* focused Shift Action Step for the last week?

....

....

....

Tell me, at what level did you honor your *Boundary* focused Shift Action Step this week?

1   2   3   4   5   6   7   8   9   10

What worked for you?   Why?
What didn't work for you?   Why not?
What do you still need to do?

....

....

....

Tell me, how did this help to support the overall development of your Vital Vision?

....

....

....

Values, Boundaries & Responsibility
Take a look at this comic strip.

Tell me, what does it tell you about responsibility?

....

....

....

Taking Responsibility

No one is perfect. In the last *Sip* you explored your personal boundary lines and how you feel when they were both respected and disrespected. You also identified your Vital Vision Boundaries that would protect your Vital Vision Values. In doing so, we focused mainly on:

- How you respected or disrespected your own boundaries.
- How others respected or disrespected your boundaries.

The truth is, of course, that there will have been times in your life when you will have disrespected the values and boundaries of others. As uncomfortable as this may be to admit, it's true for us all. To raise your value and boundary line game, it's helpful to explore times when you've behaved disrespectfully to others. We've all done it. Trust me, even I make mistakes.

Even I Make Mistakes

The comic strip at the beginning of this *Sip* is a visual example of how I can sometimes forget to honor my own boundaries. Let me tell you the story!

Beagles & Boundaries

I was staying at the home of my son and daughter-in-law while they were on vacation so that I could take care of their three beagles. Hickory, Bree, who has only one eye, and Bryson, who has only three legs. As I was preparing my bed on the first night Bree came rushing down the hallway and jumped into the bed! Did I tell you that it was only a twin bed? I got her situated only to notice that Hickory had walked down the hallway and was now peeking into the bedroom. He then backed up. I'm sure he was thinking, *what did I just see? Why is Bree in there?* He peered in again, as if to check, and then also ran and jumped into my bed! By now my twin bed was getting full. Then, you guessed it, along came three-legged Bryson! He also peered into my bedroom then walked in and took a good long look at me. I knew he wanted to be up in the bed! Of course, I picked him up and put him in the bed – leaving only a tiny space for me to sleep! All night, I grumbled about the dogs taking all the room. The next day, I discussed the matter with my son who suggested I put the dogs' beds in my bedroom. The next night, I duly arranged the three beds along the wall so that I would have room to sleep. What a relief!

Tell me, with whom was I cross? Answer: The dogs!

Tell me, with whom should I have been cross? Answer: Myself!

Insight: I was the one who had not taken the responsibility to set any boundaries!

Coffee Time!

Disrespecting Others

Tell me, when have you disrespected the values or boundary lines of another? Make notes in your journal.

Think about:
- Who did you disrespect?
- How did you disrespect them?
- How did you feel at the time?
- How do you feel today as you recall this experience?
- What would you do, or say, differently if that situation were to occur today?

Making Amends

The Shift Café Definition of Making Amends

To take the necessary steps to put right past mistakes.

Tell me, do you feel that making amends is important?

If so, why?
If not, why not?

....

....

....

How Do You Make Amends?

Sometimes my clients will choose to:

- Speak directly to the person they've disrespected to apologize
- Write a letter of apology to that person

Please note: Even if the person is no longer in your life, or has passed on, writing a letter of apology can be healing for both them and you. Try it. If writing isn't your thing, simply take yourself somewhere peaceful where you won't be disturbed and imagine yourself speaking to that person.

There are also other ways of making amends.

Tell me, can you think of actions that you can take to make amends?

....

....

....

The Shift Café Sketching Corner

Making Amends

Bring your attention to the waterfall cascading over your feet and the driftwood by your side. Draw a picture of the waterfall. Make notes on any amends you wish to make — and how. Imagine the water helping to wash away feelings of shame and guilt. Make note of your feelings.

Place this picture in your Serenity Basket.
Let the wisdom from the waterfall support your boundaries on your
Shift Café Journey.

Guilt and Forgiveness

At this point, my clients sometimes share how they feel guilty and don't know how to forgive themselves. Others speak of how they find it difficult to forgive those who have disrespected them. You will shortly explore this in *Sip 12*. For now, be proud of your courage to face these issues. It's not always easy but it will have shifted some negative energy that may have been holding you back from believing that you are worthy of attaining your Vital Vision.

The sun is now higher in the sky. You relish the cool water on your bare feet in the shallows of the lake. Close by, a hummingbird hovers in the shade of a tree. Imagine taking your gathered driftwood and writing on each one any difficult emotions, thoughts, feelings or memories that have surfaced for you while working through this chapter. Write boldly. Facing these emotions takes courage. It is this courage that will lead to the liberation of these feelings.

Nurturing Responsibility – Vital Vision Shift Action Step

Responsibility

The act of being able to accept when you have made a mistake.

Tell me, what *Responsibility* focused Vital Vision Shift Action Step will you take this week?

....

....

....

The willingness to make amends and shift thoughts and behavior.

Tell me, at what level are you going to honor your *Responsibility* focused Vital Vision Shift Action Step this week?

1   2   3   4   5   6   7   8   9   10

The courage to let go of unhelpful aspects from the past.

Tell me, how will this support the successful attainment of your Vital Vision?

....

....

....

Create a clean slate.

Serenity Basket Heart Wisdom

Reflect on this question:

From what I've learned today, does my heart have any further wisdom that will help me to attain my Vital Vision?

....

....

....

Place this guidance into your **Serenity Basket.** Let it help you on your journey through The Shift Café.

Congratulations! In this *Sip* you have:

- Explored the power of taking responsibility for past mistakes.
- Examined ways in which to make amends.

Hold on to your driftwood gently. It plays a vital role in the next *Sip* where you'll answer the question: **Tell Me**, Are You Able to Accept? Before that, we pause with the next Between the Sips where we explore how self-care can support your Vital Vision journey. I look forward to seeing you there!

The Secret of Life

by Christy Dance-Greenhut

The secret to life…it's not that hard,

You can see it while standing in any schoolyard.

Squeals of delight or a sad skinned knee,

The joy children share so openly.

Perhaps as we recover from our childhood pain.

We need to make sure the lessons remain.

Helping a friend up off the ground,

Laughing at a memory when no one is around.

Being brave enough to stand up and make a choice,

To ignore the doubt and follow your inner voice.

That's when life becomes living and so much more.

That feeling of knowing what you were truly put here for…

Thoughts become actions, small steps to start.

The doubts become distant as you follow your heart.

Dreams become reality and life starts to flow.

Seeds you've planted along the way begin to grow.

Suddenly you realize you're not just living…but living well.

You are now writing the story your legacy will tell.

There are hopes and dreams, sorrows and pain.

There's healing and blessings, and sometimes scars that remain.

But you have made it, living a life designed just for you.

Now is the time to reach out and help other's dreams come true.

#3 S = Self Care
(or lack of it)

The Shift Café Definition of Self Care

The art of lovingly nourishing your emotional, physical,
psychological and spiritual wellness so that you
become the happiest version of yourself as you
attain your Vital Vision.

It's Not Too Late.

As we age, many of us fall into the trap of letting ourselves go once we reach a certain age where we believe *I'm done* — or that society has done with us. It's hard not to feel downhearted if you realize that self-care may be way down on your priority list. Try not to worry. You're not alone. What if, however, it's not too late for you to shift into being healthy and happy again — maybe more vibrantly than ever before?

Revamping Self Care Habits

Focusing on self-care whilst journeying to your Vital Vision can bring fantastic benefits. As one of the most basic areas of self-care that many people neglect, I feel a great place to begin revamping our self-care habits is to explore our relationship with food. I'd like to share an article written by registered dietician and Holistic Health Educator, Jonathan Isbill, in which he guides you to examine:

- What you eat.
- Why you eat.
- How you eat.

Take a moment to read his article, taking note of anything that resonates with you.

Food is Medicine?
By Jonathan Isbill

Have you ever heard the phrase 'Food is Medicine'?
Well, it's not always that simple.

Food comes in many forms and flavors. It's confusing to know which foods are good, bad, or ugly. From jellybeans to lima beans, from colorful candies to fancy candlelight dinners, we use the same word, food, in each of these different settings. Are they, however, really the best foods that lead towards fully nourished and healthy bodies and hearts?

Food As Medicine

Food can be healing and nourishing to the body. Sometimes, however, it can also hurt us. I believe positive food choices play a powerful role in your thriving – especially on your quest to attain your Vital Vision.

Food is Communication

Our human body listens and learns what to do with the food we consume based on messages sent between the food and our cells. While food can nourish us from the inside out, not all food sends positive messages of health for our body and brain to grow from. If your current connection with food leaves you feeling well, I don't want to overcomplicate how you nourish yourself. However, it may be worth checking whether your relationship with the food you eat is actually triggering a roller coaster of emotions that create a lack of energy, focus and self-worth – or more.

Our Food Foundations

Food is often the first relationship you make after that with your parents. How our parents relate to nourishment tends to influence our own long-term relationship and beliefs with food. We often take as truth the smallest yet potent phrases.

'Don't eat too much.'
'Take small bites.'
'It's not proper for girls to eat that much.'
'You don't want to come across as a slob.'

Looking back as adults we may realize the hurtful, restrictive and stressful long-term damage of these phrases.

Food for Every Occasion

Food is everywhere. It's there for us when we feel sad and when we want to celebrate. It brings us together with family and friends. We can justify our pursuit of food for pretty much any reason, like taking the grandkids for ice-cream to celebrate a birthday; to encourage them after a rough week at school; or simply just to spoil them rotten. Knowing it will give them pleasure, we trust they will remember us fondly for providing that joy. Also, as adults we often go to food for pleasure, either as a reward or to soothe ourselves after feeling difficult emotions such as sadness, anger or frustration.

Food for Thought

The Shift Café Definition of Holistic Eating

Exploring how food nourishes our mind, body and
emotions so that we are nurturing our whole self.

There's nothing wrong with listening to your intuition and having a treat as part of your holistic self-care. However, with much of our modern food inventions and the busy lives we lead these simple delights become confusing and complicated. We all need nourishment yet sometimes we end up tasting the bitter guilt or shame of eater's remorse when we consume certain foods or eat too much:

I didn't intend to eat so much.
Why did I do that?
I don't feel good about myself

Food should be a valuable piece of the puzzle that leads you to wellness. Sadly, some foods, such as junk foods, make this far too difficult and can do more harm than good. Junk foods do nothing to heal or nourish our bodies. Instead, they ruin or jeopardize our chances at a healthy relationship with food, our bodies and overall wellbeing.

Me Time & Meal Time

Top Tips for Creating a Quality Relationship between Self-Care, Food & Eating.

Mealtimes are your time to really serve yourself something nourishing. Many people simply don't know how or where to begin. Below are seven simple steps that will help you develop healthy food and eating habits:

1: Create a healthy sanctuary around Me-time and Mealtime.

Remember, The Shift Café table doesn't have to just be for journaling, it could also be set for dinner! Invite friends around to share a lovely meal and decorate the table with a collection of items gathered from nature, just like I did for my Thanksgiving dinner! You have plenty of beautiful items in your Serenity Basket! There's no need for it to be a special occasion. Why not make every mealtime a special event?

2: Eat mindfully.

Take notice of enjoying your food, including flavors, textures and the experience as a whole.

3: Eat in calm, unrushed and unstressed environments.

Stressful conditions can complicate healthy digestion

4: Stick to eating whole foods.

These include: whole grains, beans, fresh fruit and vegetables.

5: Eat with others instead of alone.

Eating together increases our potential to nourish ourselves – and those we love.

6: Serve yourself a plate of grace at every meal.

Create peace, compassion and love for yourself with each meal.

7: Listen to your body.

Choose foods that heal and not harm.

Coffee Time!

Tell me, how do you currently feel about your body and general physical health?

....

....

....

....

....

....

....

....

Tell me, how did your first relationship with food begin & how does it impact your self-care today?

....

....

....

....

....

....

....

....

Tell me, what foods make you feel good about yourself and about your body?

....

....

....

....

....

....

....

....

Nurturing Self-Care – Vital Vision Shift Action Step

Self-care

The art of lovingly nourishing your emotional, physical, and spiritual wellness.

Tell me, what *Self-Care food focused* Shift Action Step will you take this week?

....

....

....

Food CAN be medicine.

Tell me, at what level are you going to honor your *Self-Care focused* Shift Action Step this week?

There's nothing wrong with listening to your intuition.

1   2   3   4   5   6   7   8   9   10

Tell me, how is this going to support the successful implementation of your Vital Vision?

....

....

....

Bring positive thoughts & feelings to the kitchen and dining table.

Self-Care Expansion

Don't forget: food is just one area of self-care. How many additional ways can you think of to bring self-care into your life? List your top three:

1.

2.

3.

Congratulations! In today's Between The *Sips*, you have:

- Examined your current relationship with self-care.
- Understood why self-care is crucial to your Vital Vision success.
- Created nourishing rituals to support personal self-care.

Remember:
> *Nourish yourself well and you will find yourself*
> *well-nourished indeed.*

We now return to your next *Sip* where you'll gather your driftwood on which you have written your difficult emotions. You'll create a healing and transformative fire as you explore more deeply where or how these difficult emotions arose. As you do so, I ask: **Tell me**, how do you feel about acceptance? I look forward to seeing you there.

When It's All Too Much

by Karen Packwood

When it's all too much, take time to ...

observe ...

... birds flying over open fields as the dawn rises over tall trees,
long grasses blowing in a refreshing breeze,
a flower opening from bud to blossom ...

listen to ...

... a brook babbling over rocks,
a child laughing in play,
you own voice in song ...

hold ...

... an autumn leaf in the your palms,
the hand of a loved one,
you own heart ...

taste ...

... your favorite fruit,
sweet honey on parched lips,
a cooling glass of mountain water ...

inhale ...

... the earth in winter...
sweet spring grass,
a rose in full bloom ...

... and know that in revealing her beauty,
Mother Earth reflects yours.

Contemplation Nook

Sip 12

Nurturing Acceptance

To forgive all is as inhuman as to forgive none.

Seneca the Younger

The Shift Café Definition of Acceptance

The knowledge that past events cannot be changed.
Understanding that the only choice you have
is how you are going to react to events.

Mid-morning at Vital Vision Lake
The Day after Thanksgiving

Place your driftwood into a neat stack. Gather damp moss to mold into a small ball of tinder. Place a small twig horizontally through your tinder and grind against a sharp rock until sparks rise. Then raise the tinder ball to your lips and blow. See how flames flicker. In the last few Sips, you've reflected on memories and experiences that may have stirred difficult emotions. Lowering the fireball into the heart of your sticks you watch as these emotions, thoughts and feelings burn.

Throughout The Shift Café journey you're constantly examining how you wish to react to complex emotions or limiting beliefs. I believe that this is all part of a healthy journey toward attaining your Vital Vision. It helps to ensure that you're creating a vision that is in true alignment with your most joyful desires. Sadly, not all people remain consistently supportive and loyal. On your journey to attaining your Vital Vision you may have experiences of feeling let down or betrayed. Perhaps, you're also carrying disappointments from earlier times in your life. Maybe these are weighing you down and preventing you from stepping fully into your Vital Vision with pride and confidence. This may certainly be the case if you have found it hard to forgive or move on from difficult times.

We hear so much about forgiveness and while forgiving others can be a good thing, true healing comes from being able to accept and release those painful events from your past, especially if they're the reason for negative self-talk and the inability to move forward. During Shift Café conversations, this topic always creates a lively debate. Letting go of past hurt and disappointment can be hard. It's easy to feel a failure. When the painful emotions arise, we beat ourselves up, asking, 'why can't I let this go?' This is the time to treat yourself with grace and compassion — just as you would a friend in similar circumstances. You may need time to mourn the loss of what once was and accept that you cannot go back and change the past.

Sometimes, however, we believe that we need to hold on to bitter emotions. These manifest as deeply rooted grudges. We somehow believe that this serves us. I'm not sure it does. To explore this from your own perspective, let your driftwood fire burn warmly beside you as you take time to examine your relationship with past hurts. To support you throughout this Sip, I ask you:

Tell Me, How Do You Feel About Acceptance?

Tell Me, How Do You Feel About Acceptance?

> ### INTENTIONS
>
> - To explore the power you have when choosing to accept that there are things from your past that cannot be changed.
> - To learn how to begin the process of accepting so that you can move forward without past hurts dominating and spoiling your life.

In the last *Sip*, you:

- Explored the power of taking responsibility for past mistakes.
- Examined ways in which to make amends.

Responsibility

The act of admitting when you have made a mistake and be willing to make amends.

Remind me: What was your *Responsibility* focused Vital Vision Shift Action Step for the last week?

....

....

....

Tell me, at what level did you implement last week's *Responsibility focused* Vital Vision Shift Step Action?

1   2   3   4   5   6   7   8   9   10

What worked for you   Why?
What didn't work for you?   Why not?
What do you still need to do?

....

....

....

Tell me, how did this help to support the overall development of your Vital Vision?

....

....

....

Accepting is a Verb

I find it helpful to remember that accepting is a verb, as in accepting the past. It's a conscious act of you deciding to let go of your anger so that the painful situation no longer controls you. When you actively choose this you begin to heal and move on from the experience.

To help you explore this in more detail, I'm delighted to share with you the following article written by therapist and coach, Linda Barbour, in which she discusses how acceptance may help us shift beyond experiences of betrayal. Although I disagree with some of Linda's views in the opening of her article, I totally agree with the rest of her opinions. As I said, this topic creates enriching and sometime challenging debates! It also teaches us that occasionally we have to agree to disagree. As you read, take note on what resonates with you. This will give you helpful clues towards your next steps for releasing suffering relating to previous experiences of betrayal and enable you to be prepared for any similar experiences that may arise in the future.

Finding it hard to forgive someone?
Try acceptance.
By Linda Barbour

Tell me, should you forgive someone?

Personally, I'm not all that big on forgiveness. I think that when I'm forgiving someone, I'm also judging. There's an implication that I'm coming from a superior place: I'm in a position to forgive you.

The Danger in Forgiveness

Forgiveness can be dangerous. When someone who shows no remorse believes they've been forgiven, they don't necessarily have to face up to the consequences of their actions. This leaves them feeling free to continue with their unacceptable behaviour. How can this be helpful? Who does it serve?

What if Someone Asks For Forgiveness?

Sometimes, however, forgiveness is possible. Imagine your husband confesses to being unfaithful and asks for your forgiveness. In doing so, he takes responsibility for his unacceptable behaviour and acknowledges that his actions were hurtful. As a result, you find yourself able to deeply forgive him. This can be powerful.

What if You Can't Forgive – Are You a Bad Person?

What if you can't or won't forgive your husband? We're told that a step towards healing is forgiveness. Finding it difficult to forgive someone can, therefore, feel like you're a bad person or somehow in the wrong. A curious thing now happens. You begin to feel terrible, perhaps even guilty, for not being able to forgive. You find yourself full to the brim of painful feelings such as hate, fear, resentment or shame. Rage turns inwards, transforming into self-hatred. What can you do to stop what has happened from eating you up and being a burden to you? What is the alternative? I believe that real peace and happiness comes from living in compassion and acceptance.

Some people struggle with the notion of acceptance because it implies that what someone did was acceptable. This is not my view of acceptance. We can accept what someone has done without condoning or agreeing with it.

When you accept that something has happened, without judgement, you can separate your feelings from someone's actions. You no longer need to feel shame, guilt, anger or hurt. While it isn't a pleasant memory, the feelings no longer burden you or cloud your current relationships.

Kat's Story

Kat looked after her partner, Gary, who suffered from dementia for many years. She felt hurt and let down by several of their close friends who chose not to stay in touch with them, including throughout the very difficult time when Gary was severely ill. Eventually, he sadly passed away. After his death, Kat picked up her old life and came into contact with these friends. She found it difficult to forget their past behaviour. She simply did not feel the same towards them. Her friends, however, said outright to Kat that she should not hold a grudge against them. They suggested that she should forgive them for the fact that they could not cope with Gary's illness.

Kat could understand that point of view. She'd also found it hard to cope. She simply couldn't forgive how they'd not been in touch at all yet now expected their friendship to continue as if nothing had happened. They even inferred that her inability to forgive was her problem. If only she would forgive them, everything could be resolved. Kat had been deeply hurt by their actions. She firmly believed that to abandon your friends at such a time was unforgivable. On reflection, she came to realise that she did not feel able to forgive them. The more she came to this realization, the more she began to criticize herself, beating herself up for being such a terrible person because she did not want to forgive them.

Eventually, she came to realize that the best and healthiest thing to do was accept the way they were. As people who cannot cope with illness and death, they avoided it. She discovered that she didn't have to waste time or energy on making judgement about them – they were not right or wrong, or good or bad. She just needed to simply accept that is how they are. She also accepted that while she felt their behaviour was unforgivable, other people may feel differently. What they had done was forgivable to them yet unforgivable to her. Once Kat had accepted both of these truths, she became clear, stopped beating herself up for not being able to forgive them and made a decision that they were not the friends she thought they were and no longer wanted a close relationship with them. She was able to let go of her judgement feelings towards them, and, more importantly, herself, and move on.

Coffee Time!

Tell me, can you think of an incident that you've found difficult to forgive? How would it feel, instead to accept the experience and let go of the anger?

....

....

....

....

....

....

Tell me, what wisdom and insights have these experiences taught you?

....

....

....

....

....

The Acceptance Process

Getting to acceptance is a must if you want to be free to walk unencumbered into your future. Without acceptance, you will continue to revisit your past instead of looking ahead to your future.

Tell me, how do you currently shift from anger, disappointment and a sense of betrayal to acceptance?

....

....

....

....

....

If you find it hard to let go of your difficult feelings when you've been hurt, perhaps you might find the processes outlined below helpful.

1: Reflection

Have a conversation with yourself or a trusted friend. Sharing your feelings and hearing them spoken aloud can be a helpful starting place.

2: Understand

Sometimes you simply have to admit that the hurtful situation happened. No matter how many times you replay it, you cannot change it. You may have to talk yourself through the decision to make healthy choices many times before you let go of past hurts — but you can do it. Give yourself grace to do so.

3: Honor

Honor what was and let go of what could have been. Often, with people who have hurt us, there are also happy and joy-filled memories. We all know that it's often the people we care for the most who also have the capacity to hurt us. Acceptance can help you look back on those happy experiences without allowing yourself to remain attached to the negative memories.

4: Empathize.

This can feel like a tough one but it can feel truly empowering and liberating. Find compassion in your heart for the person who treated you disrespectfully.

Their behavior is generally more about their past hurts and experiences than it is about you. Send them love but remember: you don't have to let them cross your 'Don't Mess With ...' boundaries and values. Nor do you have to let them become or remain in your *Shift Café Crew*.

The Shift Café Sketching Corner

Driftwood Fire

Take a moment to draw your driftwood burning in the fire.

Label with notes on each flame:
- The difficult emotions that have come up for you and the people or situations that have caused them.
- How this is impacting your attainment of your Vital Vision — both positively or negatively.
- How you are going to react: forgive, accept, both or neither? Why?

Place this picture in your Serenity Basket.
Let the transformative power of each flame support your *Shift Café* Journey.

Keep A Peaceful Heart

As you allow your emotions to evolve, expand, release or transform into forgiveness and/or acceptance, notice how your body feels. Notice your thoughts. Most importantly notice how your heart feels. As we actively engage with the overwhelming feelings relating to acceptance, we open a gateway for immense healing to occur. I certainly found this as I sat with my emotions relating to my father as my awareness of the circumstances around my heart surgery emerged. Once I decided to forgive and accept, I experienced much peace of mind and heart.

Nurturing Acceptance
Vital Vision Shift Action Step

Acceptance

*The knowledge
that past
events can't be
changed.*

Acceptance

*Coming to terms
with a fact or a
truth.*

Tell me, what *Acceptance* focused Vital Vision Shift Action Step will you take this week?

....

.... *Give yourself
grace to
let it go.*

....

Tell me, at what level are you going to honor your *Acceptance* focused Vital Vision Shift Action Step this week?

*Acceptance
is YOU
choosing to
LET GO.*

1   2   3   4   5   6   7   8   9   10

Tell me, how will this support the successful attainment of your Vital Vision?

.... *Acceptance can
open a gateway
for immense
healing.*

....

....

Serenity Basket Heart Wisdom

Reflect on this question:

From what I've learned today, does my heart have any further wisdom that will help me to attain my Vital Vision?

....

....

....

The sun is rising even higher in the sky as the driftwood flames die down. Waves lap against the shore as the ashes cool. Gather them into the palm of your hand and release them either into the gentle waves of the water, onto the soil around the roots of a tree or perhaps you may wish to climb Gratitude Hill and release them to the wind. As you do so, know that you may now have peace with these issues, experiences, memories and people. You are free to move towards your Vital Vision with a lighter heart, sense of freedom and gratitude for the wisdom these experiences have given you. The past is behind you. Before you lies a clear and joyful future.

Congratulations! In this *Sip*, you have:

- Explored the power you have when choosing to accept that there are things from your past that cannot be changed.
- Learned how to begin the process of accepting so that you can move forward without past hurts dominating and spoiling your life.

Remember:

Acceptance is the art of letting go of hurt feelings so that you can move on from the pain of the past into the joy of your future.

Now that you've examined forgiveness and acceptance, we're going to revisit Values. Often, when attempting to honor our own values, we come into conflict with others, including those we love. This often challenges everything you've explored in previous *Sips*, including your personal values, boundaries and responsibilities. Sometimes, we're also required to make decisions in relation to forgiveness and acceptance. All of this can impact on your ability to attain your Vital Vision. Therefore, in the next *Sip*, I ask you: **Tell Me**, How Do You Resolve Conflicting Values? See You There!

Forest Home

by Jennifer Corsi

I long for the song of birds
the feel of a crisp mountain breeze
the smell of the forest burning off the dew
as the sun rises over the ridge

Childhood spent in the woods
amongst the trees
remembering awakens the soul
deep down in my bones

The forest is my home
where I belong
where I come back to
the Eden I will always want.

Contemplation Nook

Sip 13
Nurturing Harmony

The goal of resolving conflict is not victory or defeat. It's reaching understanding and letting go of your need to be right.   Anon

---

The Shift Café Definition of Harmony

Heart-centered connecting, communicating
and living with others.
Loving. Listening. Respecting.

Shift

Happens

In

Fresh

Thinking...

Home
Mid-Morning - The Day after Thanksgiving

After we left the cabin last night, Bailey, Tim and I reached home, tired and content. We'd stopped by the lake along the way to watch the sleeping swans silhouetted in winter night shadows. As we cut across the snowy lawn, I wondered if the squirrel was still sleeping. Entering our kitchen, I rattled food into Bailey's bowl as Tim made us a welcome pot of coffee. The smell of pine and spruce still lingered in the air. This morning, cold ash from last night's blazing fire lies in the grate. I grab a throw from the back of the sofa and wrap it around my shoulders. 'I'll fix the fire in a moment,' Tim calls from the kitchen where he's fixing us some eggs for breakfast.

I make my way to my Shift Café table and place my father's fragile paper by my journal and sketchbook. I take out my pencils and begin to sketch. The page soon fills with images from last night. The forest, my father's cabin, Brandon's hand holding his grandfather's heart paper and flames from the fire. My heart feels peaceful.

I always enjoy the day after Thanksgiving. Reflecting on the time spent with those I love and our blessings helps me to reconnect with my love for the world in general, including those who may not be so lucky. I'm aware that not everyone is as blessed as I am and, naturally, it's not always been like this for me. I've had my fair share of trauma and difficulties such as the stillborn death of my son Ryan, being unemployed and almost penniless and my earlier marriages that ended in divorce. Yet, I know that in the grand scheme of things, I'm lucky.

A large part of that is due to my marriage. Tim and I have now been married for over thirty years and each year I realize more how lucky I am, especially as we're very different. I'm a confident, gregarious and talkative extrovert. Tim is the complete opposite — a quiet and humble introvert. Somehow, despite these differences, or perhaps because of them, we get along well.

That doesn't mean we always agree. You don't get through so many years of marriage without some conflict arising. Yet, somehow, we've found ways to negotiate these difficult moments. One thing that really helps us is that we have a shared commitment to the values by which we choose to live our life. Even then, of course, conflict can still arise. I'm sure it's the same for you. You may even find that as you venture towards your Vital Vision success, some conflict arises with those you love. It's important to know how to deal with this in a healthy, happy, balanced and respectful way. Therefore, in this chapter, I ask:

Tell Me, How Do You Resolve Conflicting Values?

Tell Me, How Do You Resolve Conflicting Values?

INTENTIONS

~⚬~✿~⚬~✿~⚬~✿~⚬~

To:

- Examine conflicts within your personal values.
- Explore conflicts between your personal values and the values of those you love.
- Create resolutions based on collaboration and priority.

In the last *Sip*, you:

- Explored the power you have when choosing to accept that there are things from your past that cannot be changed.
- Learned how to begin the process of accepting so that you can move forward without past hurts dominating and spoiling your life.

Acceptance

The knowledge that past events cannot be changed.

Remind me: what was your *Acceptance* Shift Action Step for the last week?

....

....

....

Tell me, at what level did you implement last week's *Acceptance* Shift Step Action?

Acceptance

Coming to terms with a fact or truth.

1   2   3   4   5   6   7   8   9   10

223

What worked for you?   Why?
What didn't work for you?   Why not?
What do you still need to do?

....

....

....

....

....

....

Tell me, how did this help to support the overall development of your Vital Vision?

....

....

....

....

....

....

Personal Values Conflict

The Shift Café Definition of Personal Values Conflict

A time in life when your personal values are in opposition
to the values of others – especially people you love.

When bringing your Vital Vision to life and honoring your values, you may find yourself in conflict. For example, Samantha loved attending art galleries and museums. In fact, one of her top three values was: *To live a culturally thriving life*. However, she was finding it difficult to honor this value as she lived in a small rural setting far away from the bustling city. She therefore set herself the Vital Vision to move to a thriving city where she could have easy access to a plethora of stimulating events. There was, however, a problem. Another of Samantha's primary values was: *I love my aging and disabled mother* (who lived close to Samantha in her rural location) *and want to spend quality time caring for her.*

Samantha felt torn. Both of her values felt crucial, yet one was holding her back from honoring the other. You'll find out how Samantha resolved this conflict shortly. Before this, however, I want to share with you two common questions that are often raised with me when I discuss values with Shift Café readers or workshop participants. I think it's helpful for you to examine these questions before delving more deeply into conflicting values so that you are clear in your mind why respecting your values is important.

1. Do I have Values?
2. Are Values Selfish?

Do I Have Values?

Joseph, a man in his early thirties was in the process of divorcing his wife with whom he'd grown apart. Leaving her in the family home with their children, he was now living temporarily with friends and sleeping on their sofa. As we were discussing his values, he told me, 'I don't think I have any values. I'm just in survival mode.' However, as we worked through the *Don't Mess with …* exercises in *Sip 9*, he began to see that his decision to end his marriage had come from the impulse to honor subconscious values that included:

*   *Don't Mess* with my mental and emotional wellbeing.
*   *Don't Mess* with honesty.
*   *Don't Mess* with loyalty.
*   *Don't Mess* with vows and promises.

Joseph's wife had involved herself in activities that, for him, did not honor the values with which he had come into the marriage. His decision to divorce her was his way of not only valuing his values but also recognizing and honoring his own right to live a happy life. Slowly but surely he was able to:

- Know and respect his values, specifically in relation to relationships.
- Understand that he had done the right thing.
- Release guilt he was carrying in relation to breaking up his children's home.
- Recognize that he was acting as a positive role model to his children demonstrating that personal values are a right to be respected even if they initially create discomfort for others.

Looking back over the previous few years of his marriage, he realized that he had spent much of them self-sacrificing and denying his values. This simply resulted in a sense of bitterness and deep unhappiness. These feelings lifted as he came to understand how honoring his values were a vital component of his mental and emotional self-care.

Are Values Selfish?

Perhaps the most important question of all! By striving to honor your personal values, do you risk becoming egocentric and uncaring? As you work through this *Sip*, I invite you to consider this. I've already introduced you to Samantha. You will shortly meet Bill. Both experience conflict between their personal Vital Vision values and those of family members they dearly love. Notice how, in the end, they both value the need for collaboration and agree to let go, to some degree, of their vision for the greater good of their whole life. I'm sure this will resonate with you and that you'll find it helpful as you shift towards resolving value conflicts in your own life.

Conflict with Others

Sometimes, of course, not only do we find ourselves in a state of inner conflict but also in conflict with the values of others such as our children, partner or the wider family. I often find that clients are keeping themselves from honoring their values precisely due to this type of conflict. As with many things in life, there are times where we are called to collaboration. For example, Bill was happily married to Claire yet yearned to travel and live abroad. One of his core Vital Visions was: *To live an open-minded life.* This was because he valued *learning, in person, from a wide variety of cultures.*

For Bill, this included long-term traveling and living among these cultures so that he could gain an integral understanding of their traditions. However, having two school-aged children, Claire's Vital Vision included: *I want to live in a stable home location.* This was because she valued the notion of her daughters being able to maintain consistent and loyal friendships. She believed, and the girls were in agreement, that this might be difficult if they were constantly traveling. Clearly, within the family, individual values were in conflict.

Coffee Time!

Examining Conflict and Values in Your Own Life

Tell me, do any of your personal values clash, with one preventing you from honoring the other?

- Which values are they?
- What is the conflict?
- How does this feel?
- How do you think this conflict can be resolved? (Don't worry if you can't think of any answers, I will help you resolve this later in the *Sip*.)

....

....

....

Conflict of Values with Those You Love

Tell me, do any of your personal values clash with the needs of others, especially those close to you?

- What are the values?
- What is the conflict?
- Who are you in conflict with?
- How does this feel?
- How do you think this conflict can be resolved?

....

....

....

....

If you're stuck on how to resolve this conflict, try this next activity.

The Power of Collaboration — Vision and Value Conflict Resolution

---

The Shift Café Definition of Collaboration

To work jointly with others towards a
mutually agreed goal.

'I got what I wanted, only better because I got
things that I didn't even know I wanted.'

Here's how I advise you to tackle conflicts in relation to values.

1. Take an overview of the whole situation.
2. On a Scale of 1 – 10, put the conflicting visions in to an order of desire and priority. Here's how this worked for Samantha.

	Value	Vision	Conflict
Samantha:	1: *To live a culturally thriving life.*	*To live in a thriving city with access to theaters, museums, galleries etc.*	
	2: *I value my relationship with family and love my mother.*	*To care well for my mother.* Her mother lives in a rural setting and has no desire to move. Plus: Samantha wants to live alone in the city.	*In order to live in the thriving city, I will have to leave my mother, yet I also want to be close to, and care for her.*

When Samantha thought honestly about the order of her priority for these values, she knew that her top value tugging at her desires was her yearning to move to the city yet, by taking an overview, she was able to see that her aging mother was a priority. She decided to work out ways in which to stay living in the rural location to care for her mother but in such a way that she could take regular short trips to the city. Her solution? She decided to hire a residential nurse once a month to live with her mother for long weekends. During this time she would have fun in the city. By identifying this conflict, Samantha was able to find a way to honor and respect both of her values.

This was much the same for Bill. Once he'd taken an overview of the situation and listened to the values and desires of his wife and children, he agreed to put his extended travelling desires on hold until the girls had left school. Although he found it hard to deny his personal values, he understood that another of his values, *to love and support his wife and children to the best of his ability*, needed to be his current main focus. In gratitude for this collaboration, his wife and children happily agreed to accompany him on adventurous vacations to locations they would not normally visit. This included a memorable horseback trip in Mongolia.

Roles

You can see how different roles in life played an important part in the lives of both Bill and Samantha, even though their individual family circumstances were quite different. These roles became especially important in times of values conflict and resolution. In making his choice to delay his traveling desires, Bill decided to honor his role as a father. Samantha was in conflict with her role as a single woman yearning for adventure and her role as a daughter. You'll be aware that you have a range of roles in your life. For example, my core roles are wife and mother. Additionally, I also value my role as a servant leader where I focus on supporting others so that they can achieve above and beyond expectations in life. For the success of your Vital Vision, it's helpful to be clear about both your roles and values in life.

Tell me, can you outline your roles in the following areas?

- **Family**
  Role

Intention/Desire within that role:

....

....

....

- **Friends**
  Role

Intention/Desire within that role:

....

....

....

- **Community**
  Role

Intention/Desire within that role:

....

....

....

- **Globally**
  Role

Intention/Desire within that role:

....

....

....

Current Conflict of Values

Tell me, do you have any current areas of conflict relating to your values in relation to your Vital Vision?

....

....

....

Value Conflict Resolution

Tell me, thinking about your specific roles, how can you create collaboration to ensure that your values, and the values of those you love, are respected?

....

....

....

....

What Have You Learned?

Tell me, do these ideas differ from ways you have handled conflict in the past. If so, how?

....

....

....

....

Moving Forward

Tell me, how might you handle values conflict moving forward, especially when you think about attaining Vital Visions?

....

....

....

....

A movement catches my eye through the window. Wisps of gray smoke from your fire are curling up through the trees above the summit of Vital Vision hill into the white sky. I imagine you crouching by the lake and letting go of all unhelpful conflict or unhappy feelings raised in previous Sips. I trust that the calm of the deep lake water and the heat of the flames are transforming any pain, sorrow, heartache or grief associated with these painful issues so that you're able to step into your Vital Vision confidently and happily. I watch until smokes ceases knowing that as the ashes cool you'll be releasing and scatter these past hurts. I imagine how peaceful your heart now feels.

The Shift Café Sketching Corner
What does your heart look like?

Take a moment to draw your heart, or an image from nature that represents your heart. Label with notes on any positive feelings your heart currently feels in relation to creating harmony around conflicting values.

Ask yourself: how can I maintain these feelings while stepping into my Vital Vision?

Place this picture in your Serenity Basket.
Let the wisdom from your heart support your Shift Café Journey.

Nurturing Harmony - Vital Vision Shift Action Step

Heart-centred
connecting,
communicating
and living with
others.

Loving
Listening
Respecting

Tell me, what *Harmony* focused Vital Vision Shift Action Step
will you take this week?

....

Do you
have
values?

....

....

Tell me, at what level are you going to honor your *Harmony* Shift Action Step
this week?

1   2   3   4   5   6   7   8   9   10

Are values
selfish?

Tell me, how will this support the successful attainment of your Vital Vision?

....

....

Harness the
power of
collaboration

....

....

Serenity Basket Heart Wisdom

Reflect on this question:

From what I've learned today, does my heart have any further wisdom that will help me to attain my Vital Vision?

....

....

....

Place this guidance into your Serenity Basket. Let it help you on your journey through *The Shift Café*.

Congratulations! In this *Sip*, you have:

- Examined conflicts within your personal values.
- Explored conflicts between your personal values and the values of those you love.
- Created resolutions based on collaboration and priority.

Remember:

For the success of your Vital Vision, it's helpful to be clear about both your roles and values in life.

It's fair to say that in recent *Sips*, you've worked exceptionally hard, digging deep into some tough subject matter. It's very important that alongside this, you know how to respect and support yourself. Therefore, in the next *Sip*, I ask you: **Tell Me**, How Do You Reward Yourself? See You There!

Top Dumble

by Lynne Doshi

Released from lead my Spitz sprints to the start
past bonfire circles that have scorched the land
leaving village, school, lanes, cottages that mark
medieval pastimes and Byron's age,
barks at a man for elderflower gathering,
impatient at my ambling down the field.

Hawthorn tango with trees unlike the field
an artwork of rapeseed yellow, the start
of which will end with the August gathering
of green harvesters vibrating the land
steep slopes that rise merging with other age
old crops that oxen in ridges mark.

My dog sniffs the birch, leaves his scented mark.
The Woodland Trust's Bonney Doles grassy field
beds great burnet, harebell, oaks young in age
beside wizened apple trees that start
at the wind's touch and girls walk the land
hazelnuts pocketed, for the hay gathering.

Brambles boast purpling pearls for gathering,
the ripest blackberries the blackbird's mark.
Biscuit head for the steel bridging the land
between wild meadows where owls hunt the field
mouse and calloused hands pick cowslips to start
winemaking in pre-industrial age.

Rushing stream plashing clear through the Ice Age
Dumble, just right for sploshing and gathering
pooh sticks to race from the deep valley's start.
Fungus frilled logs and Mercian mudstone mark
the finish; folk carouse Cowslip Sunday in the field,
iron hooves and hobnail boots print the land.

His pawprint trail enters ancient woodland
where crusty lichen, moss velvet and age
old ivy stippled wych elm, oak ask, field
maple to conceal the Green Man gathering
Gaia's guardians to protest the mark
of men precipitating the earth's start.

The yellow mark arrows the final field,
cows graze land and we circle to the start
of the dog show, a heritage gathering.

Contemplation Nook

Sip 14
Nurturing Celebration & Reward

Do not spoil what you have by desiring what you have not; remember that what you now have was once among the things you only hoped for.
Epictetus

The Shift Café Definition of Reward

The celebration you gift yourself as you complete
each Shift Action Step – no matter how small.
Relax. Reflect. Reward.

Bees & Mid-afternoon Relaxation at The Shift Café Apple Orchard

With the picture of your heart stowed firmly in your Serenity Basket, you leave Vital Vision Lake following a track behind a group of hickory trees that leads into an apple orchard where snow-laden branches are currently empty of fruit or flowers. It brings comfort to know that in the stillness of these winter months, Mother Earth is making her preparations for the forthcoming blossoming. When this happens, the lake will have thawed and the cool winter sun will have transformed into the heat of summer.

The Shift Café Orchard

Look at this image of The Shift Café orchard in summer.

Imagine yourself there in the summer walking over a newly cut lawn and taking your seat at a freshly set table in the shade of the trees. The sweet smell of apple blossom and brewing coffee fills the air. Sipping your coffee you delight in watching bees buzz from one blossom to another, noting how they nuzzle into the heart of the flowers to gather their pollen.

As one particularly diligent bee retracts and prepares to hover to another blossom, you notice how hundreds of white pollen particles cover its entire body. It surely received a great reward for its hard work. In turn, we receive great reward from their hard work, not only in the sweet honey they produce but also the work they do to keep our food sources plentiful and our planet balanced and harmonious. When able to work in harmony with the flowers and trees rooted so firmly in Mother Nature, the bee's actions bring great rewards to us all. Mother Nature does her job well.

For us humans too, it's now well known how time spent with Mother Nature nourishes and enhances our well-being. Sitting here, you're surrounded by a great bounty of natural goodness. This in itself is rewarding and is all freely available to you. Yet, often, we're too busy to appreciate these gifts. How often do you consciously take time to appreciate the hard work of nature? How often do you consciously take time to appreciate your own hard work and reward yourself for your efforts? How good are you at celebrating achievements? We're often so focused on the doing, giving, supporting and achieving that we forget to celebrate ourselves. I'm also guilty of this. Therefore, in today's Sip, I ask:

Tell Me, How Do You Reward Yourself?

Tell Me, How Do You Reward Yourself?

In the last *Sip,* you:

Harmony

Heart-centred
connecting,
communicating
and living with
others.

- Examined conflicts within your personal values. Explored conflicts between your personal values and the values of those you love.
- Created resolutions based on compromise and priority.

Remind me: what was your *Harmony* focused Shift Action Step for the last week?

Loving
Listening
Respecting

....

....

....

Tell me, at what level did you implement last week's *Harmony* focused Shift Step Action?

1   2   3   4   5   6   7   8   9   10

What worked for you?   Why?
What didn't work for you?   Why not?
What do you still need to do?

....

....

....

Tell me, how is this going to support the successful implementation of your Vital Vision?

....

....

....

....

....

....

....

....

Relax. Reflect. Reward.

I'm sure you'll agree that the last few *Sips* have been jam-packed with challenging information and activities. This can feel exhilarating. It can also feel uncomfortable, overwhelming and exhausting. In this *Sip,* you're going to relax a little and have some fun – yet fun that is also of paramount importance.

As with any journey where you're practicing new skills, it's vital to find ways to stay motivated so that you can stay on track. I truly believe that the joy you receive from noticing how each shift enhances your life and naturally leads to an even greater shift will feel rewarding. However, it's also helpful to give yourself additional boosts along the way.

As I go about attaining each new shift in my life, I may have a specific reward in mind for when it's complete. For example, I might plan a special road trip with my husband so that we can enjoy some quality time together. Alternatively, I might set aside some time to indulge in one of my favorite hobbies and paint a picture. I recently asked participants in my workshops how they'd like to reward each new shift. attained. Here's what they suggested:

A walk in nature	Baking and eating a cake with friends	Beginning a new embroidery	Buying and reading a new book	A glass of bubbly!	A box of chocolates
Treating myself to a new item of clothing/jewelry	Spending an afternoon sketching/painting	Visiting a friend	Phoning a friend	Spa Treatment	Dancing
Massage	Gardening/Visiting a garden center	Going to see a movie	Going out for dinner	Cooking a nice dinner at home	Hair Cut
Booking a short trip away	Visiting a museum/art gallery	Taking the dog/children/family out for a special walk/picnic	Singing	A long, lazy bath	Visiting a market/beach

False Rewards

When I hold Shift Café conversations on the topic of rewards with workshop or program attendees, I often discover that many of them view a reward as a treat such as a slice of cake or a bag of chips. After eating them, however, they feel guilt and remorse. The treat became something that triggered negative feelings about themselves and was, therefore, not a true reward! Rewards should always feel nourishing!

This always creates powerful 'aha' and breakthrough insights with participants realizing how they were fooling or tricking themselves. Sabotage at its best! Once they became aware of this, great strides were made in thinking of healthy, happy and nourishing rewards that truly felt like a celebration. These became a vital part of each participant's Shift Café Vital Vision journey.

Coffee Time!

Top Ten Rewards.

Tell me, how do you reward yourself?

Write your Ten Top Rewards in the box below.

Remember – these do not have to be expensive or cost money. For example, one of my favorite rewards is to spend time playing with Bailey, my adorable dog.

1	2	3	4	5
6	7	8	9	10

The Shift Café Sketching Corner
Reflect

Now that you've delved deeply into how you reward yourself, look at the outline below of an apple tree from The Shift Café's very own orchard. See the table overleaf to discover how each component of the tree relates to your Vital Vision journey. Using the information in the table, color each component of the tree and make notes on your Shift Café hurdles, shifts and transformations so far.

Place this picture in your Serenity Basket.
Let the wisdom from the apple tree support your *Shift Café* Journey.

Component of Tree	Represents Your:
Roots:	Values
The hollow in the trunk:	Fixed mindset - Obstacles that still need to be overcome.
The trunk:	Growth Mindset - Innate gifts and skills that provide the resilience to shift from fixed to growth mindset.
Branches:	Boundaries - A clear-cut line (boundary line) around your Vital Vision Values that you don't cross. Nor do you allow others to cross them.
Apples on the branches:	Vital Vision - (hopes/dreams/aspirations)
Falling apples from left of tree:	Release - Letting go of anything that doesn't serve the attainment of your Vital Vision.
Falling apples from right of tree into The Shift Café's Serenity Basket:	Wisdom - Growth attained, success reaped, knowledge attained, steps taken towards attaining your Vital Vision.
The Shift Café's wildflowers:	Self-Love - Nurturing and celebrating each shift towards attaining your Vital Vision – no matter how small.

The Shift Café Wishing Well

In the corner of the orchard there is a well. Once used to draw fresh water for the inhabitants of the house and to water the café gardens, it has now turned into a Wishing Well where passers-by love to cast coins into its depths and make a wish.

Cast Your Wish

Tell me, if your heart could receive the greatest of all rewards for attaining your Vital Vision, what would it be? You could even ask your heart:

> 'What is it that you wish for me so that I may
> become truly happy?'

....

....

....

....

....

....

....

....

....

....

Congratulations! You now have a very clear idea of how you will reward your success! Make sure to include them after every Shift Action Step has been attained!

Nurturing Rewards - Vital Vision Shift Action Step

Reward

*The celebration
you gift yourself
as you complete
each Shift Action
- no matter how
small.*

*Allow your
finances to
support your
Vital Vision.*

Tell me, what *Reward* focused Vital Vision Shift Action Step will you take this week?

....

....

*Relax
Reflect
Reward*

....

Tell me, at what level are you going to honor your *Reward* focused Vital Vision Shift Action Step this week?

*Give yourself
boosts along the
way.*

1   2   3   4   5   6   7   8   9   10

Tell me, how will this support the successful attainment of your Vital Vision?

....

....

*Rewards should
always feel
nourishing.*

....

Serenity Basket Heart Wisdom

Reflect on this question:

From what I've learned today, does my heart have any further wisdom that will help me to attain my Vital Vision?

....

....

....

Place this guidance into your Serenity Basket. Let it help you on your journey through *The Shift Café*.

Congratulations! In this *Sip*, you have identified your Top Success Rewards!

Remember:

> *As with any journey where you're practicing new skills, it's vital to find ways to stay motivated so that you can stay on track.*

Hopefully, you've now realized the amazing work you're undertaking in *The Shift Café* and have identified some great ways to celebrate each success along the way – no matter how small. Of course, I also realize that you might have identified some Shift Action Steps that you have not successfully attained. Equally, you may fear that you're not going to attain you Vital Vision. If this is you, hang tight as I deal with this in the next *Sip*, where I ask you: **Tell Me**, Are You Open to the Power of Possibilities? See You There!

The Shift Café
Nurturing your wisdom, intelligence, beauty and spirit — one sip at a time.

Something More

by Christy Dance-Greenhut

There were things she hadn't accomplished – yet.
Many years ago she'd set them aside. It had been a choice–not a regret.
She'd loved those years she'd spent teaching others to mountain climb.
Then one day she woke up to her inner voice saying:

This is Your Time

She felt unworthy and small, standing at the bottom of her mountain side.
Courage and clarity left her–choosing to hide.
Yet she knew that her something more was waiting at the top.
She wanted deeply to go, even as self-doubt told her to stop.

The Task is too Large.

Who was she to think she could make that climb?
She had no energy, no plan–and no time.
Then one tiny daisy came into view.
It seemed to be saying:

This Step is For You

That one small step gave view to another,
Then three more steps decided to uncover.
Some were smooth and easy to take,
Others so rough, she feared she'd made a mistake.
These were the ones that took such great focus that it came as a surprise,
When the top of the mountain appeared before her eyes.
Her view of the world was now much larger
than it had been a short time before,
She celebrated the daisy that lead to the steps,
that led to her ... *something more.*

Contemplation Nook

Sip 15
Nurturing Possibilities

It does not matter how slowly you go, so long as you don't stop.

Confucius

The Shift Café Definition of Possibilities

~ꝏ~ꝏ~ꝏ~ꝏ~ꝏ~ꝏ~

To be open to an array of creative solutions.

Mid-Afternoon on Vital Vision Hill.
Eagles & Hickory Trees

Leaving the orchard behind, you take up your Serenity Basket and saunter towards the base of Vital Vision Hill. Winding through a thicket of tall hickory trees you pass through a rickety gate that's almost falling from its hinges. A sudden motion from the canopy of a nearby tree distracts you while climbing over a fence. You can hardly believe your eyes. High in the tree's canopy, the white head and yellow beak of a bald eagle protrudes from branches where it's layering twigs to make a nest. What a sight! In just two or three months, as late winter will turn to spring, tiny eaglet chicks with bills open wide will receive hunks of flesh from recently snagged fish offered from their mother.

Mesmerized, you slowly lower to your haunches. Losing your balance, you fall towards the Serenity Basket causing its contents to clash loudly. Mother Eagle freezes – alert to you. What will she do? There are a number of possibilities. It is the same for you. As you've sipped your way through this Vital Vision journey, you've already been met with choices and obstacles that may have rattled you. Each came with a range of potential outcomes. Sometimes, however, we become stuck. Really stuck. How do you respond? Do you give up or do you search out the many creative possibilities open to you? In this Sip, we explore this as I ask:

251

You'll discover that the answer lies in a single word.

Tell Me, How Do You Nurture The Power in Possibilities?

INTENTIONS

To explore:

- The Power in Possibilities.
- How you can apply this to your Vital Vision.

In the last *Sip*, you:

- Explored rewards.
- Identified your success rewards.

Reward

The celebration you gift yourself as you complete each Shift Action Step — no matter how small.

Remind me: what was your *Reward* focused Shift Action Step for the last week?

....

....

....

Tell me, at what level did you implement your *Reward* focused Shift Action Step?

1   2   3   4   5   6   7   8   9   10

What worked for you?   Why?
What didn't work for you?   Why not?
What do you still need to do?

....

....

....

Tell me, how did this contribute to the success of your Vital Vision?

.... *Reward*

.... *Reflect*

.... *Reward*

Sensing that you mean no harm, Mother Eagle continues creating her nest. In a few short weeks, following the incubation and hatching of her eggs, she'll be preparing her fledglings to become independent and leave. She does so in stages, initially by bringing their food to a place outside of the nest so that they have to literally fly in order to eat and, therefore, survive. In the preceding weeks, she'll have taught them how to spread their wings, letting the air levitate them from the nest floor. Within this safety, they practice the skills that will take them on to the next stage of their journey. Does this come easily to them? No. At times they struggle. They have to practice, adjust, make mistakes and become accustomed to a more independent mode of existence — new ways of thinking and being. Sometimes they will fail. They have to take part in their own journey from the fixed to growth mindset.

In many ways, I think Mother Eagle plays a similar role to the members of your Shift Café Deluxe Delight Crew. If you remember, a crucial purpose of your Deluxe Delight crew is to help when you're caught in the grips of:

I can't ...
I'm stuck ...
I don't know how ...
I failed again ...

Clearly, the Deluxe Delight crew is a valuable asset and tool helping you to shift from a fixed to a growth mindset — especially when you're stuck. Today, you're going to explore this more deeply and come to understand what I mean by *The Power of Possibilities* and how this can be an equally valuable tool. We begin by examining a concept many people feel nervous to explore.

Failure

Throughout your time in *The Shift Café*, you haven't, yet, explored failure — specifically, the power of failure. When things seem impossible and you actually find yourself literally failing, or feeling as if you're about to fail, just as some of those fledgling eaglets might feel as they learn to fly, this is the perfect time to fail with confidence – knowing that this becomes an opportunity to reframe. People who look at things from a growth mindset see failure as a form of development. That's a really powerful shift, sometimes a difficult one. However, the reality is that often it's within these failures that the golden kernels of success are waiting. When you're really struggling with something, it can actually mean that you're heading towards a fundamental breakthrough.

Thanks to the work of psychologist Carol Dweck, I've discovered that often all it takes to help create this breakthrough is the introduction of one simple word into your vocabulary: YET. Dweck discovered that placing the word yet within this mindset process is powerful. I've also found this to be the case. When I talk with people who are feeling stuck, I'll say, *'you're telling me that you don't know how to do this – yet?'* Immediately, they agree, *'yes, that's right.'* I then take it to the next level, *'we know you don't know this yet, so what is your very next step?'* When you say the word yet, everything shifts.

Although it's a tiny word, yet is powerful. It implies that you can get better in the future, thus opening the door to new and powerful possibilities. It becomes the trigger word to help you to instantly take some tiny steps away from your fixed mindset towards your growth mindset.

The Shift Café Definition of YET

A simple word that implies that anything can work out better in the future. The door is always open to new and powerful possibilities.

During the Shift Café Deluxe Delight Crew *Sip*, you focused on:

I can't …
I'm stuck …
I don't know how …
I failed again …

Notice how this changes, simply by adding the word yet:

I can't … yet.
I don't know how … yet.

I'm stuck yet I know my saucer crew member can help me.
I failed again yet if I reflect on what went wrong, I'll find a way to try again.

YET = **Y**es!
Eventually
Triumph happens!

Can you see how the power shifts? Ultimately, YET is encouraging. I was recently reminded of this when I took up Spanish classes with my husband, Tim.

A Spanish Tale
Shifting from Yikes to Yet

Last year, Tim and I decided that we wanted to learn to speak Spanish so that we could converse with the Spanish-speaking members of our community in Arizona. We signed up for several different courses. The first was to last for three or four weeks, the next would entail four or five weeks of study. We attended all of the first lessons and worked really hard, practicing between classes. It didn't take us long, however, to exclaim, 'Yikes! We're in way over our heads.' We therefore attended only two of the second set of classes before proceeding to say, 'Yikes! We can't keep up!' Our home practice conversations went something like this:

Me: *Can you do this?*

Tim: *No.*

How are you feeling?

Dumb.

I'm sure other people in the class are getting it.
Maybe we haven't practiced enough?

In order to help us, I bought a flip chart, writing notes all over it. I hung it from the back of our bedroom door. You can imagine the scene. There were the numbers: *uno, dos, tres.* I had notes on how to pronounce the vowels. The months were listed yet I still thought *yikes, I'm not keeping up.* I would look at the notes, thinking, *there's too much, I can't get it.* Interestingly, we were out eating dinner one evening and met a couple of ladies who were in our class. They came over to speak to us:

'You're in our class!'
'Yes! How are you doing?'
We can't do it!' Relieved, Tim and I agreed. 'We can't do it either!'

We completely dropped out of the third class before we'd even begun. I couldn't help my fixed mindset limited thinking:

I knew we couldn't do this.
Why did we try this?
We should have begun this a long time ago.

A few days later, we were driving through the mountains when I heard a radio advertisement for a language learning App. *Okay,* I thought, *I want to explore this.* I enjoyed taking part in their three free lessons realizing how effectively it imparted the knowledge. I then signed up for their full class. This App enabled me to shift from the fixed mindset, *I don't know how to learn Spanish and I never will,* to, *I don't know how to speak Spanish ... yet.* Tim and I would have felt a lot better if we'd claimed **yet** earlier.

After several moments of patiently building, Mother Eagle flies off to collect more twigs to strengthen the walls of her nest. Grateful for having witnessed this sight, you continue on your way noticing how the higher you climb the cooler it becomes. Mother Nature, it occurs to you, fully understands the power of possibilities in yet. Imagine if, in the deep of this winter, she were to say 'I haven't grown any crops.' What if she left it at that? We all depend on Mother Nature to say, 'I haven't grown any crops yet.' Even though that seems impossible when it's freezing and there's snow on the ground, we know she will soon create new growth. Mother Nature is saying yet all the time. Nature contains constant change and constant potential. As do you.

Coffee Time!

How can yet expand your Power of Possibilities and support the attainment of your Vital Vision?

YET:

- Creates *permission* to relax on the journey towards attaining your Vital Vision.

- Creates *trust* that you will eventually become successful in the attainment of your Vital Vision

- Inspires *hope*.

- Creates *confidence*.

- Creates *space* for small, yet determined, steps in the right direction.

- Allows *expansion* and *evolution* of your Vital Vision—perhaps to shift beyond what you initially believed possible. I call these Bonus Shifts. You'll be exploring these in the next *Sip*.

Tell me, can you think of any other ways in which yet can support the attainment of your Vital Vision?

....

....

....

The Power of YET Mantra
Helping you shift from Yikes to YET

Remember:

YET = **Y**es!
Eventually
Triumph happens!

I love the above mantra and use it each time I begin a new Vital Vision. Here are three more great examples created by participants during a recent Shift Café workshop:

YET
You
Evolving Over
Time

Yield!
Enter!
Triumph!

Yikes!
Everything is coming
Together!

Tell me, what is your personal YET mantra?

YET = **Y**.....

E.....

T.....

If you allow it, this mantra can become another powerful tool of support and encouragement on your journey to attaining your Vital Vision. To aid this, write this powerful three-letter word on sticky notes and put them all around your personal Shift Café Contemplation Nook and home. Make sure to include them in places where you'll see them, whether you're washing dishes, getting dressed in the morning or before you go to bed at night. You need the word yet. It reframes. It implies: I can get better. Ultimately, it opens a door to a million possibilities. That's powerful.

Harnessing the Power of Possibilities in YET.

Tell me, do you remember how the wildflowers at the base of your Shift Café tree represented self-love? **Remind me**, how did you identify self-love for yourself?

....

....

....

Tell me, has anything shifted for you in relation to self-love?

....

....

....

The Shift Café Sketching Corner

What's waiting in The Shift Café Flower Meadow?

As the eaglets are hatching next spring, flowers will be spreading new blooms in the heart of the wildflower meadow. In The Shift Café flower meadow, yet awaits. This yet represents each of the potential yets that you'll need to stretch towards during this winter and into next spring as you attain, and stretch beyond, your Vital Vision.

You may, or may not, know the required next steps. It doesn't matter. Simply color yet. As you do so, allow yourself to come to a place of peace and acceptance with the idea that everyone has to deal with many yets on their journey to success. Sometimes it's easy. Sometimes it's hard. Sometimes you do it alone. Sometimes you have others to accompany you along the way. Reflect and make notes on any thoughts or feelings that arise for you. Feel free to add more self-love wildflowers!

Place this picture in your Serenity Basket.
Let the wisdom with each flower support your Shift Café Journey.

Nurturing Possibilities – Vital Vision Shift Action Step

Tell me, what is your *Possibility* focused Shift Action Step for this week?

You Evolving Over Time.

....

....

....

Tell me, at what level are you going to honor your *Possibility* focused Shift Action Step this week?

1	2	3	4	5	6	7	8	9	10

Yikes! Everything is coming Together!

Tell me, how is this going to support the development of your next Vital Vision?

....

....

Yield Enter Triumph

....

Serenity Basket Heart Wisdom
Reflect on this question:

From what I've learned today, does my heart have any further wisdom that will help me to attain my Vital Vision?

....

....

....

Place this guidance into your Serenity Basket. Let it help you on your journey through *The Shift Café*.

Not so long ago, bald eagles were on the brink of extinction due to hunting and pollution yet now they are flourishing again. Somehow, even on the brink of extinction, possibilities were created and nurtured to save and protect them. Don't let your dreams become extinct. Open up to the possibilities so that you can make them happen. On the cusp of returning to the summit of Vital Vision Hill, stay focused and keep your eyes eagle sharp. Then swoop on your vision, grab it with the deftness with which an eagle snags a fish to feed its young knowing that their survival depends upon it.

Congratulations! Once again you have worked hard! In this *Sip*, you've explored:

- The Power in Possibilities.
- How you can apply this to your Vital Vision.

Remember:
> *Nature contains constant change and potential. As do you.*

You're almost at the end of your Shift Café journey. In this *Sip*, you've opened yourself to a world of new and creative possibilities. We're shortly going to expand this further in your final *Sip*, as I ask you: **Tell Me**, What are Your Bonus Shifts? See you there!

The Shift Café
Nurturing your wisdom, intelligence, beauty and spirit — one sip at a time.

Unfinished Sculptures

by Shama Padalka

We toil and turn
We sizzle and burn
We hardly ever rest
Even after a test
Coz there's a chapter new
And quizzes with some cue
We handle all
We never stall
We are unfinished sculptures

We're diamonds rough
Yet to face chisel and buff
We absorb like a sponge
Always ready to take the plunge
Are we ready? Are we done?
Mature and trained all in one?
Are we there yet?
Or are we still
Your unfinished sculptures?

Between the Sips
The M.O.S.T common reasons cited for not stepping into your Vital Vision.

#4 = Time

As adults, we often juggle our time caring for others, sometimes feeling as if we have no time for ourselves, especially when it comes to investing time in improving our own personal well-being. Does this resonate with you? If so, allow yourself to create a moment to read this article by Caribbean based wife, mother of three and Attorney-at-Law, Angelina Lee in which she explores her own relationship with time. Take note of anything that resonates

I Made Time
By Angelina Lee

I woke up early this morning and couldn't go back to sleep so I decided to get out of bed. As I sat in the living room and slowly sipped my morning coffee, I looked out the window and marveled at the peaceful stillness of nature in the overcast morning light. When I finished the contents of my cup I continued to sit and look outside. It was still early. I had time.

Or did I?

Quiet Time

All at once, I could think of the many things I had to do. This quiet time would be optimum for me to concentrate on something that I've been putting off for lack of space to really think and create. There were toys on the floor from last night that should have been packed away before bedtime. I thought of how I'd been meaning to start gentle exercise in the early mornings in order to kick-start my day. This was my chance. There is also a bread recipe that I want to try. Perhaps I would start kneading the dough now so that we could have fresh bread with breakfast. Then, in an instant, I decided that I would not get up from the couch – yet. I knew once I got up, I would likely be on my feet for the better part of the day. I decided to sit there a little longer. I had time.

Or did I?

Within moments, I found myself reaching for my phone to check my email. Thankfully, I caught myself and stopped. Why did I feel the need to fill every moment of my day with something that had to be done? Yes, I could think of ways to fill these few quiet moments, but did I really need to? What if I looked at spending quiet time just being with myself as something important – as something that also needed to be done? It is something that needs to be done.

Self-Love Language

I often say that silence is my self-love language. In silence I breathe deeply and my depleted reserves are restored. In silence I connect with myself and check in with how I'm really feeling. In silence I honour my need for moments of stillness and allow my busy mind to rest a little while. Silence speaks. It tells me that:

> I don't have to rush.
> There is always time.
> I am enough, just as I am, regardless of what I do or leave undone.

And so, I simply sat there and looked outside.

> I breathed.
> I connected.
> I rested a while.

Making Time

I was reminded that sitting in silence isn't a waste of time; it slows time. If we wait until we have time, it will never happen. We have to make time. There will always be something to do. But we need to create time to be.

> Time to be silent, still – at rest.

That's what I did this morning. I stopped debating whether or not I had time. And, instead ...

> I made time.

Coffee Time!

Tell me, how do you feel about gifting time to activities that nourish and enhance your personal dreams?

....

....

....

Tell me, which specific aspects of your Vital Vision require more time?

....

....

....

Tell me, how could you create more time for yourself to attain your Vital Vision?

....

....

....

Nurturing Time - Vital Vision Shift Action Step

Many of us feel guilty for taking time to devote on our dreams, as if we somehow don't deserve them.

Does this resonate with you?

Tell me, what *Time* focused Shift Action Step will you take this week?

....

I don't have to rush.

....

....

Tell me, at what level are you going to honor this Shift Action Step in the coming week?

1   2   3   4   5   6   7   8   9   10

Tell me, how is this going to support the successful implementation of your Vital Vision?

....

I breathed.
I connected.
I rested a while.

....

....

Remember:

We now turn to your next *Sip* where we will gather at the base of the hickory tree in *The Shift Café* garden where I ask you: **Tell Me**, What are Your Bonus Shifts? See You There!

The Shift Café
Nurturing your wisdom, intelligence, beauty and spirit — one sip at a time.

Grace

by Karen Packwood

... deer bounding silently through forests,

a cat stretching after a deep sleep,

sunlight shining through stained glass,

the first sight of spring cowslips,

daisies dancing in a wild meadow,

nettles blooming beside dock leaves,

crows building nests in canopies of leafless trees,

a robin trilling in winter,

a dog bounding unleashed along a beach,

a child at peace,

waves lapping on a shore lake reflecting the rays of a full moon,

a campfire glowing under a starry sky ...

take a moment ...

... appreciate your moments of grace.

Contemplation Nook

Sip 16
Nurturing Bonus Shifts

When a man has said, 'I have lived!' then every morning he rises is a bonus.

Seneca

The Shift Café Definition of Bonus Shifts

The positive and unexpected additional shifts & gifts
that emerge as you journey towards your Vital Vision.
They expand, bringing additional joy & success
to your process and outcome.

Vital Vision Hill
Late Afternoon
Apple Blossoms, Mushroom & Butterflies

You rise and continue your saunter to the summit of Vital Vision Hill. Squirrels leap from branch to branch of the hickory tree. The sun is high. The time will soon come where its warmth will be strong enough to melt the packed snow and fresh water will cascade into Vital Vision Lake. Spring energy will arrive in Gratitude Valley and the ground underfoot will become cornfields and open meadows. The sweet aroma of field daisies will dance on the breeze as they brush against your legs. You reach the summit with ease. Like your purpose and vision in recent weeks, your gait has become strong. Although you may not yet have attained all that you wish, you know in your heart that you are close – perhaps closer than you have ever been.

Turning to look back over the Shift Café Gratitude Valley, you see every nook and cranny of the landscape you've explored on this journey including how, in the forest, you explored your growth mindset, by the lakeshore you created your boundaries and, in the apple orchard, you decided how to celebrate and reward yourself. Perhaps, most importantly, you've learned to listen to your heart. There is, however, still one uncovered area yet to explore. A final question to come with your final Sip:

Tell Me, What Are Your Bonus Shifts?

Tell Me What Are Bonus Shifts?

INTENTIONS

❦ ❦ ❦ ❦

To identify:

- Your personal Shift Café Bonus Shifts.
- The unexpected positive outcomes for those you love – and beyond.

In the last *Sip*, you explored:

The Power of Possibilities

- The Power in Possibilities.
- How you can apply this to your Vital Vision.

To be open to an array of creative solutions.

Remind me: what was your *Possibility* focused Shift Action Step for the last week?

....

You

Evolving

....

Over

Time.

....

Tell me, at what level did you implement your *Possibility* focused Shift Action Step?

Yield!

Enter!

Triumph!

1   2   3   4   5   6   7   8   9   10

What worked for you?   Why?

What didn't work for you?   Why not?

What do you still need to do?

....

....

....

Tell me, how did this contribute to the success of your Vital Vision?

....

....

....

The Gifts in Bonus Shifts

I've learned that every Shift Café journey always provides the most surprising bonus shifts, including for me. Do you remember that I earlier mentioned how influential my grandmother had been whilst growing up? This came as a bonus shift discovery for me while writing this book as it also helped me examine my views on acceptance. Until then, I'd viewed her as quite a harsh lady who had, on many occasions, appeared cold to me. This was especially the case following the birth of my son Brandon. One day I was preparing to visit him in hospital following a difficult and potentially life-threatening birth. My grandmother telephoned to say, 'Don't get too attached. That way, when he dies, you won't feel it so badly.'

I was shocked, of course, but was also used to such harshness. It was only while paying attention to the four M.O.S.T common obstacles as they relate to my life, and understanding the difference between forgiveness and acceptance, that I've been able to view my grandmother's harshness from a different perspective. I took time to learn more about her as a woman exploring how she too had suffered her share of pain and suffering, including the death of her own son when he was just eight months old. Naturally, I now realized that her comments about not becoming too attached to my son were actually intended to be protective. She didn't want me to suffer as she had should Brandon not survive. Taking this time to reflect allowed me to shift my mindset — and heart. As I did so, something wonderful happened. Repressed and unvalued memories re-emerged of precious time spent with my grandmother. I gained a whole new appreciation of the legacy she had gifted to me while still alive.

Grandma's Legacy

As a young girl, my grandmother and I would spend much time walking in the meadows around my home. Striding along, she would point out the names of the many wildflowers: 'See, this is a fern getting ready to unroll' or 'that's a May Apple, that's a Trillium.' To this day, thanks to my grandmother, I can remember all their names.

On other walks, in spring, she would take me to the woods where we would hunt for edible mushrooms growing around the roots of dead trees. Sometimes it was easy to find them, other times we had to steadfastly forage

under dead leaves or through overgrown grass. I still recall the smell of dank earth and unexpected fluttering of butterflies that we unwittingly disturbed – not to mention the delicious taste of our mushroom hoard.

As I recall these experiences and relate them to the journey of attaining a Vital Vision, a similarity strikes me: among wildflowers and dead trees, there are often elements of beauty that remain unnoticed unless you consciously seek. Yet, they exist. When you have the good fortune to come across them, it adds a bonus to your experience. This is the same on your journey towards your Vital Vision. Along the way, there have been many hidden bonuses. Let's explore.

The Path is Not Always Easy

I like to think there are two potential routes to attaining your goals. The first is how people often expect it to be. They hope it will be a gentle stroll through rolling meadows until they easily, and free of panting breath, reach the summit of their Vital Vision Hill. You now know that not many journeys work out this way. I feel this is a good thing. When you take this route you miss much of the potential beauty of your journey — even if the alternative route is more slippery.

The Slippery Route

Fixed mindset detours and fears lead you through the wintery routes of ice and thawing snow that may cause you to slip. However, if you wrap up warmly, take the time to pause and observe remaining silent and calm, hidden beauty will be revealed. It might begin as you have done on your journey, with spying the track of a deer, sitting by waves lapping gently on a shore or noticing a bird's nest high in a tree.

If you pause long enough and pay even closer attention, the beauty expands. A deer track becomes the track of a mountain lion. The bird's nest becomes a family of fledglings taking their first flight. These things you may have missed if the winter ice and snow hadn't slowed your journey. These are your Bonus Shifts. It's often in these slippery moments, while connecting with your Bonus Shifts, where life enhancing breakthroughs occur. Your fears thaw and you begin to flourish – and so does your Vital Vision.

Sarah's Story

Sarah is currently in graduate school. Her Vital Vision was to attain a job that she felt passionate about on graduation. Despite applying diligently for many jobs, she had received rejection after rejection. At the beginning of the Shift Café program, she was feeling demoralized and hopeless. Yet each week, despite a heavy college timetable, she turned up for the weekly Shift Café conversations. Sometimes she was only able to listen as she was driving to school. Sometimes she joined from her car in the university parking lot before attending lectures. Other times, she joined from her home office in between writing essays due for imminent submission. Regardless of obstacles, Sarah showed up.

Each week, she would share how she had received another rejection. She was stuck in a bind of being over-qualified for some jobs and under-qualified for others. However, as the conversation evolved, and she got to know and build trust with her fellow Shift Café members, she began to share more of her dilemmas and desires. Did she want to have higher pay even though it meant doing a job she loathed, or did she want to pursue a passion project even if the pay was less? Family expectations were demanding the former yet Sarah's heart was with the latter. It was during a breakout conversation in the Shift Café that Sarah shared a crucial piece of information that was to transform her Vital Vision accomplishment. Sarah was discussing how she felt stuck in this bind between being under-qualified and over-qualified. Her Shift Café crew member, Teresa, asked her, 'In what way are you under qualified? What's missing?'

Sarah: *I don't have enough experience with 3D printing.*

Teresa: *Could you volunteer with a company that specializes in 3D printing so that you can place that experience on your resume?*

Sarah*: (after a slight pause for thought) I've actually invented something to be printed 3D.*

Instantly after sharing this, Sarah had a life transforming 'aha' Bonus Shift light bulb idea:

I could ask my professor if he would let me create this within the department.

By the time the Shift Café crew had met the following week, Sarah's professor had agreed to create her 3D Printing invention AND she had secured a passion project job. She was eight weeks into the Shift Café program! Grab your coffee! Let's now begin to uncover your Bonus Shifts.

Coffee Time!

Identifying Your Bonus Shifts

You're now entering a process of deep reflection. Consciously aligning with alert awareness of, and gratitude towards, your Vital Vision bonuses allows for a greater evolution of your Vital Vision. In its turn, this allows for life enhancing shifts on a personal level as well as for those you love–and beyond.

Reflecting on Your Vital Vision

Unscrewing the thermos taken from your Serenity Basket, the rich aroma of coffee fills the air. In the distance, under the heavy branches of the Hickory Tree, you see your Shift Café Deluxe Delight crew gathered around your Shift Café table. They're waiting for you to join them. They wave and smile. You wave and smile in return while silently sipping your coffee. You'll join them soon enough but first you take time to cast your eye over Gratitude Valley and back to your original Shift Café Vital Vision.

Remind me, what was it?

. . . .

. . . .

Vital Vision
a dream that

. . . . *your heart yearns*
to attain.

. . . .

Tell me, how has it changed?

Success

....

Attainment of

.... *your Vital*

Vision to a level

that feels

.... *rewarding.*

Tell me, have you attained all/some/none of it? No negative judgments, just an honest reflection.

Mindset

....

Your beliefs

that affect how

.... *you choose to*

think, feel, and

react to any

.... *situation.*

rewarding.

Tell me, what three emotions define your progress thus far?

-

Tell Me,

-

How does
your heart feel?

-

Take another sip of your coffee as you observe and listen. The dank smell of mushrooms nestled in tree roots fills your nostrils. Torrents of water from Release Falls cascade into Vital Vision Lake. Recall your difficult emotions carved onto driftwood and remember your Value Leaves that were gathered in the forest outside my father's cabin. Take a moment to appreciate all that you've gathered in your Serenity Basket. What Bonus Shifts have each of these blessed you with – not only for you personally but for those you love and, perhaps, the world.

The Shift Café Sketching Corner
Your Personal Bonus Shifts

Color this apple blossom. Each petal represents one of your personal bonus shifts.

Label each one with notes on:

- Your Bonus Shifts.
- Their positive impact on your life beyond your Vital Vision.
- How this will influence you moving forward.

Place this picture in your Serenity Basket.
Let the wisdom on each petal support your
Shift Café Journey – and beyond.

Your Bonus Shifts for Those You Love

Color these edible mushrooms. Each one represents a bonus shift that you've created for those you love.
Label and make notes.

- Who have you helped?
- How have you helped them?
- How will this influence you moving forward?

Place this picture in your Serenity Basket.
Let the wisdom on each mushroom support your
Shift Café Journey – and beyond.

Your Bonus Shifts for Those Beyond Your Immediate Circle

Color the butterfly. Each wing represents a bonus shift that you've created for those in your wider community, even globally. As yet, they may be unseen to you. Simply take some time to reflect on what you would like them to be.
Label your pictures and make notes

- Who have you helped?
- How have you helped them?
- How will this influence you moving forward?

Place this picture in your Serenity Basket.
Let the wisdom on each wing support your
Shift Café Journey – and beyond.

Reflect and Prepare

The late afternoon sun is lowering, your breath hovers in the air. You rise and walk across Vital Vision ridge as night mist begins to descend. Ahead of you, on the ledge, you see the hazy outline of a deer, poised and alert. A small robin perches on antlers held proud. For a split second you all freeze before the deer bounds away causing the robin to soar into flight. From the ledge, you recall bald eagle's nest high in the hickory trees, hares nibbling winter grass, squirrels gathering nuts, herons catching fish, smoke curling from fires and ice beginning to thaw–making way for spring.

In the last light of day, the blue heron swoops low over the lake's surface sending circular ripples across the lake. Balancing confidently on one leg, it focuses towards the horizon where the first rays of moonbeams shine on thawing ice. In the shimmering of the moonlight the lake's surface becomes like a mirror reflecting back to you all that you have achieved on this journey through The Shift Café. No matter how complete or incomplete, a sense of accomplishment beats in your heart. The moonlight becomes brighter, the vision on the lake's surface stronger. You are now able to see your current vision and beyond this to a vision you've not yet been able to imagine. This is the vision of your future now that you know the pathway of listening to your heart and accomplishing your dreams.

Tell me, what can you see? What is your ultimate Vital Vision?

....

....

....

Tell me, who does it serve?

....

....

....

Tell me, why is it important?

....

....

....

Celebrate and Reward

You silently thank the heron for helping you find this Vision and head back to the Shift Café table where your crew greets you with loving embraces and a fresh pot of steaming coffee. The night sky is lit with lanterns whose flickering candles are reminiscent of dancing fireflies. As the day sets over your completion of The Shift Café journey, the full moon radiates. It's been a good winter. You now know that for as long as you live, you'll always be able to find your light in any darkness and to survive any bitterly icy winter until the thaw gives way to the new life of spring. All it takes is to have a clear vision, to know your values and to have the courage to journey with a growth mindset so that you can step into one Shift Action Step at a time. And don't forget to always remain grateful and give yourself grace.

Reward & Celebrate

You have accomplished so much.
Tell me, how are you going to reward yourself for these accomplishments?

Reward

The celebration you gift yourself as you complete each Shift Action Step – no matter how small – and attain your Vital Vision ... ... and beyond

....

....

....

Shift Café Heart Promise

> ### A Shift Café Heart Promise
>
> An expression of gratitude and love to your own Inner Wisdom and Mother Earth – and a commitment to always honor them.

As one journey completes and another begins I invite you, if this fits with your values, to create a Shift Café heart promise. Within this promise allow yourself to consider and include elements of:

♡Gratitude   ♡Recognition   ♡Appreciation

Christy's Shift Café Heart Promise

Here's an example that Christy, a former Shift Café participant, shared with me:

My Shift Café Heart Promise to Myself

I promise to serve myself as well as others.

I promise to speak as kindly to myself as I do others.

I promise to be open and honest.

I promise to be as determined to find myself as I
would be if I were searching for a lost child.

I understand I may be that lost child.

I promise to believe that I truly do have the ability
to step into the Power of my Potential.

I promise to be grateful every day – and love my heart along the way.

From your Inner Wisdom, request any support you still require. Write for yourself, those you love and beyond.

My Shift Café Heart Promise.

....

....

....

With immense love, gratitude and respect, place a copy of this promise into your Serenity Basket.

My Hope for You

My hope for you is that you'll be blessed with the confidence and courage to know that you can attain, and carry forward, anything you wish. I'm not speaking here of materialistic gains, I'm speaking of the gifts of your Spirit and how you will spread these gifts as seeds among your community, especially to those most in need.

As you gather together with the gifts of courage, truth, wisdom, and integrity you will scatter them far and wide, planting Shift Café wildflower meadows and orchards of love so that all who come into contact with you, all who drink coffee with you, will be blessed with similar gifts to those that you have received along the way. This will be your legacy to the world.

Congratulations! This week, you have identified:

- Your personal Shift Café Bonus Shifts.
- The unexpected positive outcomes for those you love – and beyond.

Remember:

You now know that you will always be able to find your light in any darkness, to survive any bitter and icy winter until the thaw gives way to the new life of spring.

Although we have come to the end of this stage of your journey with *The Shift Café*, your journey is far from over. Perhaps it is only just unfolding.

With that is mind ...

Nurturing Your Bonus Shifts & Ultimate Vital Vision Shift Action Step

The positive and unexpected additional shifts & gifts that emerge as you journey towards your Vital Vision.

They expand, bringing additional joy & success to your process and outcome.

Tell me, what is your Ultimate Vital Vision Shift Action Step for this week?

....
♡Gratitude
♡Recognition
....
♡Appreciation

....

Tell me, at what level are you going to honor your Ultimate Vital Vision Shift Action this week?

Be blessed with confidence and courage.

1   2   3   4   5   6   7   8   9   10

Tell me, how is this going to support the development of your Ultimate Vital Vision?

....

Listen to the gifts
....
of your Spirit.

....

Serenity Basket Heart Wisdom

Reflect on this question:

From what I've learned today, does my heart have any further wisdom that will help me to attain my Vital Vision?

....

....

....

Place this guidance into your Serenity Basket. Let it help you on your journey through *The Shift Café*.

Thank you for joining me on this journey.

I wish you the very best as you journey towards the expansions of all your Vital Visions.

Much Love, Cindy

BUTTERFLY

by Andrew Roberts

Do we awake daily
into the Abyss of
a mystical dream?

Do the doorways to
distant galaxies
await us when we
look to the stars
that dance to the
enchanting music
of the midnight sky?

Or do they sleep
blissfully
within the tiny
wings of the
sweet and gentle
butterfly?

Glossary

Term	The Shift Café Definition
Acceptance	The knowledge that past events cannot be changed. Understanding that the only choice you have is how you are going to react to the events.
Authentic	The courage to live a life true to your own needs and desires regardless of what others may think, say, or do.
Between the Sips	An opportunity to pause between the main Sips so that you can focus on common limiting beliefs and actions that prevent you from attaining your Vital Vision.
Bonus Shift	The positive and unexpected additional shifts and gifts that emerge as you journey towards your Vital Vision. They expand bringing additional joy & success to your process and outcome.
Boundary	A clear-cut line *(boundary line)* around your Vital Vision Values that you don't cross. Nor do you allow others to cross them.
Breakthrough	An instance of achieving a vital insight that creates solutions to a situation that feels stuck.
Coffee Time	A period of quality time within each Sip devoted to guided activities that will bring your Vital Vision to life.
Collaboration	To work jointly with others towards a mutually agreed goal.

Term	The Shift Café Definition
Comfort Zone	A feeling of psychological, emotional, and physical safety.
Connection	The ability to open your heart and attend to the needs of another from a place of love – and to be able to receive this love.
Contemplation Nook	Your own private Shift Café haven within your home or garden.
Don't Mess With	Your hard lines in the sand that no one is allowed to cross.
Dream	An unfulfilled desire that your heart yearns to bring to life.
False Reward	A token or word of praise given without any real meaning behind it.
Fixed Mindset	A rigid mindset that is not open to new information or alternative possibilities.
Golden Obstacles	Opportunities that are disguised as obstacles; you actively work towards releasing or transforming them.
Gratitude	A feeling in your heart that has nourished and enhanced your sense of wellbeing and wisdom – and, often, others too.
Gratitude Journal	A written list of everything, from the smallest to the largest, for which you feel gratitude throughout the day.
Growth Mindset	A mindset that is constantly open to new levels of learning, developing and understanding.

Term	The Shift Café Definition
Harmony	Heart-centered connecting, communicating and living with others. Loving. Listening. Respecting.
Heart Wisdom	The hidden truth held deep in your heart.
Holistic Eating	Exploring how food nourishes our mind, body, and emotions so that we are nurturing our whole self.
Inspiration	To be stimulated and motivated to create life enhancing shifts by the creativity and wisdom of others and your own heart's desires.
Inspirational Hero/ine	A person who lives their life in a way that inspires others to be more intentional in their own life.
Internal Monologue	The internal negative loop in your mind that often affects the way we see others and ourselves.
Legacy	What you gift to others so that they can achieve.
Legacy Seeds	Positive deeds we do, with love, for others who will remember these acts. In turn, they'll pass them on to others.
M.O.S.T.	Common reasons for not stepping into your Vital Vision: Money. Overwhelm. Self-Care. Time.
Making Amends	Taking the necessary steps to put right past mistakes.

Term	The Shift Café Definition
Mindset	The beliefs and thoughts that affect how you choose to feel and react to any situation.
Nurturing	To mindfully attain your life's dreams by nourishing them, and yourself, with loving kindness, and compassion.
Personal Values Conflict	Times when honoring one of your values causes you to break another one of your values.
Positivity	Creating and maintaining an optimistic mindset when shifting through challenges as you attain your Vital Vision.
Possibilities	To be open to an array of creative solutions
Reflection	The ability to look at your own actions, thoughts and beliefs with honesty & integrity so that you can show up in life for yourself, and others, at the highest and most enjoyable level.
Responsibility	The act of being able to accept when you've made a mistake. The courage to let go of unhelpful aspects from the past. The willingness to make amends and shift thoughts and behavior.
Reward	The celebration you gift yourself as you complete each Shift Action Step.

Term	The Shift Café Definition
Sabotage	The act of spoiling a longed-for accomplishment.
Self Care	The art of lovingly nourishing your emotional, physical, psychological, and spiritual wellness so that you become the happiest version of YOU as you attain your Vital Vision.
Serenity Basket	A precious basket holding your collection of nature gifts that represent the wisdom guidance and memories deep within your heart.
Shift	A conscious movement away from aspects of your life that no longer serve you in order to welcome life enhancing experiences and feelings that do.
Shift Action Step	An expression of gratitude & love to your Inner Wisdom and Mother Earth – with a commitment to always honor them.
Sips	Chapters of The Shift Café.
Success	The attainment of your Vital Vision to a level that feels rewarding.
Super Deluxe Delight Crew	Your chosen community of high quality, trustworthy and supportive people, activities, locations, and pets

Term	The Shift Café Definition
The Shift Café	A serene space for quality time & gentle reflection so that you can work out what gentle shifts you need to make to improve your life.
Values	A meaningful set of rules guiding your life choices.

REFERENCES

Carol S. Dweck, Ph.D. 2007. Mindset: The New Psychology of Success (New York: Ballantine Books).

Acknowledgements

When first viewing a book in a bookshop or library, your eye may be curiously drawn to the name of the author. You imagine them writing alone until, at some point, the final sentence is written and they can rest their pen (or close their computer lid) and relax. The truth is, of course, different. For a book to become cohesive and enjoyable, the author must allow their initial speck of an idea – their Vital Vision–to be supported by a team of experts offering guidance throughout the writing period. While creating *The Shift Café*, I'm blessed to have collaborated with a wonderful team of family, friends, experts and contributors who I would like to thank.

Thank you to the team at The Spirit Spa Press™ for ensuring this project remained creative and fun throughout the whole process.

Thank you Karen Packwood for your skillful co-writing, editorial and project management skills – and friendship!

Thank you Emily Woodthorpe. What can I say Emily!? Your illustrations are stunning and deeply enrich *The Shift Café* experience. It has been a Deluxe Delight to work with you!

Thank you Tara-Lee York for your patient and diligent typesetting and graphic design skills. You are the calm ship navigating stormy seas.

Thank you to Christy Dance-Greenhut for contributing your amazing gifts of creativity, kindness, humor and compassion to the editorial team. I am truly grateful!

Thank you to the inspirational members of my primary pilot study group for the first version of *The Shift Café* manuscript: Lesley Chenoweth, Tiffany Dover, Colette Durham, Sarah Franklin, Christy Greenhut, Chris Kevitt, Tara-Lee York, Shama Padalkar and Lesley Reuter.

Thank you to the amazing women who became the secondary pilot study group for the final version of *The Shift Café* manuscript: Lauren Burton, Deena Elmore, Susan Kayser, Joyce Kleinman, Charity Lewis, Priscilla Scalf and Jennifer Schall. **Thank you** for your heartfelt and honest feedback relating to each *Sip*. You all helped to shape *The Shift Café* and I trust many will benefit from your words of wisdom.

Thank you to my early readers, Pam Holt and Charity Lewis. Wading through an undeveloped manuscript while juggling hectic work and/or family life while home-schooling during a pandemic is no mean feat. Your honesty relating to the boring bits was immensely helpful!

Thank you to my wonderful *Shift Café* crew members and dearly loved friends, Kathy Adams and Marilyn Clark who undertook various proofreading tasks along the way to publication, giving honest feedback and moral support!

Thank you to my mentor Jane Powers for your coaching which saw the creation of some of the text used within *The Shift Café*.

Thank you Eric Lofholm for your inspirational coaching and for granting me permission to use your empowering Level 10 game.

Of course, *The Shift Café* would simply not have been possible without the loving support, memories and inspiration of my family.

Thank you Great-Aunt Florence, (Yelton, née Muck), for your lessons of strength, courage and open-heartedness. They created a lasting legacy on my life.

Thank you Louis Winn – my grandfather. Your love of lifelong learning and personal development inspired me greatly.

Thank you Mary Winn (née Muck) – my grandmother. You taught me the ways of the forest that became a lifelong love and source of sustenance.

Thank you Ruth Winn (née Wright) – my mother. Your deep love has stayed in my heart forever, as has all that you taught me about the art of stoic perseverance, resilience and having friends of all ages.

Thank you Doug and Yvonne Winn – my brother and sister-in-law. The memories shared over the years have greatly influenced aspects of this work.
Thank you Brandon and Heather – my son and daughter-in-Law. Thank you

for always being ready to undertake research, chat through ideas and offer unconditional support while creating memories around fires as fireflies danced.

Thank you Tim, my husband, soul mate and best friend who, for the last thirty-four years of marriage has patiently supported every Vital Vision I've yearned to attain – no matter how crazy they may have been. The day I met you, my life shifted for the better helping to make me a happier person. Thank you, Tim, for being there for me while creating *The Shift Café*. I feel deeply grateful for your gentle kindness, tolerance and love – and for supplying me with endless cups of coffee!

And finally, Kenny Winn – my father. **Thank you** for carrying my heart in your pocket for all those years.

Thank You!

Thank You to *The Shift Café's* talented content contributors for granting permission to quote and reproduce poems and articles. **Thank you**, to the technical team at The Spirit Spa Press!

Illustrator

Emily Woodthorpe is an illustrator and writer based in Nottingham, UK. She studied Illustration at the University of Lincoln before completing a Masters in Creative Writing at the University of Nottingham. When she's not drawing or writing, she's sipping tea while engrossed in a good book. She can be found at: emwoodthorpe.wordpress.com.

Typesetter and Graphic Designer

Tara-Lee York is a Graphic Designer based in New Brunswick, Canada who specializes in graphic, web and UX design services with a focus on book design, responsive websites and mobile apps. She lives in a homestead with her husband and five children. In her spare time, she loves to care for her animals and tend the land. She can be contacted at: www.taraleeyork.com.

Poets

Jamie Cloud is a writer and teacher based in China. He grew up in Texas where he studied theater before teaching English in China and earning his MA in Creative Writing at the University of Nottingham, UK. He finds inspiration in stories that have embedded themselves in the consciousness of their respective cultures, from the works of Shakespeare to the American western to any number of fairy tales, myths and legends around the world. Jamie can be contacted at: jamiewcloud@yahoo.com.

Jennifer Corsi is a woman un-afraid of taking big leaps in life. She loves deeply, adventures often and seeks to profoundly experience our world with her husband and two children.

Christy Dance-Greenhut is a former teacher based in Hope, Indiana. She is now living her best life as a published poetess! As a graduate of *The Shift Café* Train the Trainer program, Christy uses her creativity, joy and loving compassion to help spread Cindy's *The Shift Café* message. She adores supporting those who feel stuck, lost or hopeless as they SHIFT into the POWER of their POTENTIAL!

Lynne Doshi has a M.A. (Dist.) in Creative Writing from the University of Nottingham. She was an English teacher at secondary school (high school) level for over thirty years. Lynne has also trained as an actor and storyteller, performing at venues and events across Nottinghamshire.

Teo Eve is a poet, short story writer, and member of GOBS Collective, based between Nottingham – a UNESCO City of Literature – and London in the UK. Teo's story "To Be Seen" won Nottingham UNESCO City of Literature's "My Voice" competition, and Teo's debut poetry collection THE OX HOUSE is forthcoming from Penteract Press July 2022. Teo can be found on Twitter @teo_eve_

Zarley Lawson is a poet based in Athens, AL. He first started writing poetry to help with his personal emotions. His initial passion for poetry came from his grandmother who he considers his heroine and guardian angel. In his free time he enjoys writing poetry, cooking, spending time with friends and family and helping with The Boy Scouts of America as an Eagle Scout mentor.

Shama Padalkar is an educationist, artist, a people connector and an entrepreneur. She has been a program chair and lecturer at graduate and post graduate levels for most of her career. She loves to read, travel, learn and teach fine arts. Now a US citizen she helps Indian diaspora settle in a foreign culture. She is well connected with all local non profit organizations and is currently on the board of directors of 'Just Friends'. As a conversationalist she has led several discussions on diversity and inclusion, and happily engages in any dialogue on her background and culture.

Andy Roberts is a Nottinghamshire based poet who has a passion for writing about the beauty of nature and the cosmic energy that surrounds us which makes all sentient life forms equal. This philosophy is also reflected in his work as a Spiritual Medium. More of Andrew's poems can be found on Facebook as "The Mystic and the Muse".

Between the Sips and Acceptance Articles

Linda Barbour is a Therapeutic Coach based in Suffolk, UK. Blending psychotherapy with coaching, she helps clients to recognize and interrupt old patterns of behavior and replace them with new and better ways to succeed in their personal or professional lives. In her spare time, Linda loves to ride her horse in the countryside surrounding her home. More information about Linda can be found at: www.lindabarbour.com

Astra supports her Soul-Led Entrepreneur Tribe in creating more health, happiness, wealth and freedom in their businesses and lives. She spends her own free time relaxing as much as possible, cuddling with her fur babies, hanging with her human and spreading Animal Kindness across the land. You can reach Astra and follow her on social media via her website at: www. AstraTheShaman.com

Angelina Lee is a wife, mother of three and Attorney-at-Law from a small island in the Caribbean. After her Plan A life left her wanting more, she is now exploring her Plan Be in which she tries to live more intentionally: a plan with less doing and more being. She enjoys sharing her insights and learnings on her blog: exploringplanbe.com

Jonathan Isbill is a Registered Dietitian, Health coach, educator, and writer who holds a Master's in Nutrition and Dietetics from Ball State University. He first began his journey learning about food as medicine in search of answers to help heal his mother's Crohn's Disease during high school, which led him to discover holistic and functional medicine. Jonathan is a passionate advocate for nutrition, education, and helping others better understand how to live their best lives possible. You can connect with him further by signing up for his weekly weekend newsletter on Substack or connect with him on social media and say hello!

Cindy Allen Stuckey MEd MSM

Tell me, for what is it that you yearn?

Cindy Allen Stuckey – *The Shift Café*

Featured in O, the Oprah magazine, Entrepreneur, Fortune and Forbes, Cindy is an international speaker, coach and educator whose mission is to serve people determined to create positive changes in their lives. As the first-ever female Director at Knauf Insulation of North America, she was responsible for Human Resources and Organization Development. She is now founding President and CEO of Making Performance Matter® – home of *The Shift Café™*. *The Shift Café*, where women who drink coffee together change the world, leads you on a creative pathway to self-discovery that helps you identify what you want in life, why you want it, and, most importantly, HOW to develop the courage to achieve it. Cindy believes in your POTENTIAL to live your best life - now. To do this, you need to CREATE a shift. This SHIFT begins with you.

The easiest way to connect with Cindy is to join her life changing Shift Café conversations on facebook that are dedicated to helping you SHIFT into the POWER of your POTENTIAL.

Facebook: The Shift Café with Cindy
Website: www.cindyallenstuckey.com
Email: cindy@makingperformancematter.com

Karen Packwood BA(Hons) MA PGCE

When the wild one within calls, listen, for she might just be about to change your life.

Karen Packwood – How to Survive When Life Falls Apart™

Based in the U.K, Karen graduated with Distinction from the MA Creative Writing program at University of Nottingham. Specializing in writing for wellness, she is the co-author of three #1 best selling books. Karen is also founder and Creative Director of The Spirit Spa Press™, an independent publisher of authors who help readers improve the quality of their emotional, physical, psychological and spiritual wellbeing. Additionally, Karen is Director of The Spirit Spa Writers' Sanctuary™ where she hosts *Soul Walks and Sacred Circles™* writing retreats in the heart of rural England, internationally and digitally. Alongside this, Karen is currently a Ph.D. creative writing researcher at the University of Nottingham, UK.

The easiest way to connect with Karen is through her YouTube channel where she creates content dedicated to supporting people in the early stages of recovering from a nervous breakdown so that they can understand why the breakdown happened and decide their next natural steps towards recovery.

YouTube: https://www.youtube.com/c/KarenPackwood
Website: www.karenpackwood.com
Email: karen@karenpackwood.com

Legacy

by Christy Dance-Greenhut

My gift to the world, my legacy,
it's a constant, ever changing, part of me.
I won't leave a statue or a portrait in the museum of art,
instead I hope to leave a thousand pieces of my heart.
I hope those I love still hear me saying, I Believe in You,
and that it gives them the courage to make their dreams come true.
I hope I'm that whisper, perhaps even a calming voice,
that helps them find peace when they have to make a difficult choice.
I hope I've set the example to show kindness to all,
and shared with them my struggles, even after a fall.
I hope they've seen me rise and find a different way,
to start again, to find the hope and beauty of each new day.
I can't claim these values simply as mine alone,
I was gifted along the way by the angels I have known.
I've borrowed parts of their legacy to pass along to you,
and I hope that I've left you something that you can borrow too.

Step into the POWER of your POTENTIAL.
The SHIFT begins with YOU.

Are you ready?